Song in a Strange Land

Sacred spaces = places of feasting p 7
Holy Week + Easter + suff of women p 8
Julian of Norwich p 18

D1564642

Song in a Strange Land

The Wellspring Story and the Homelessness of Women

Rosemary Haughton

Templegate Publishers
Springfield, Illinois

Copyright © Rosemary Haughton

All rights reserved. Except for brief passages quoted in a newspaper, magazine, radio, or television review, no part of this book may be reproduced in any form or by any means, electronic or mechanical, including photocopying and recording, or by any information storage and retrieval system, without permission in writing from the publisher.

ISBN 0-87243-188-6

First Published in the United States by
Templegate Publishers
302 East Adams Street
P.O. Box 5152
Springfield, IL
62705-5152

TABLE OF CONTENTS

Dedication

This book is first dedicated to all of the Wellspring people, past and present, who created it by what they were and are, by their questions and their friendship.

I owe especial thanks to Nancy, whose criticism improved the book enormously, and to Ruth, who patiently typed it not once but three times, deciphering my personal hieroglyphics without the aid of the Rosetta Stone!

I owe a wide debt of gratitude also to those in my 'pre-Wellspring' life who brought me where I am, but most of all to the members of my family, with all their ups and downs, their disasters and triumphs, their rage and grief and hope and love, and their huge capacity for living.

INTRODUCTION

MARCH 1990

This is the eighth spring since seven of us came to this house in pursuit of a dream. This summer we celebrate eight years in the house. Outside, the snow is melting and soon the shoots of spring bulbs will appear. Inside, the bulbs grown in bowls have symbolized the possibility of spring, and now, their flowering over, they wait to be put in the ground, where they will flower again, even this year.

While we wait — and work — for the garden to bring forth its new shoots and flowers we grow bulbs in the protection of the warm house, hoping that, once transplanted, they will soon flower again from deeper roots. The work of Wellspring is rather like that. In the protection of this place, women whose lives have never been allowed to grow, or whose roots have been torn up, come here. Security and friendship allow them to put down a few roots and to grow, and later, in homes of their own, they hope to settle and find security and grow to blossom.

Is it possible? Can homeless women truly put down the deep roots that allow full and strong growth and the unfolding of blossom and fruit? Looking around, it is so obvious that fullness of growth is something few women come to. They are constantly uprooted, they are clipped and trained to special purposes, they struggle in tiny patches of scanty soil. The blossoms open and then fall, frosted before the fruit can form. They have no secure place, the good earth is not theirs.

Soon we shall celebrate the Passover, a simplified ritual for all kinds of people, filling the chapel — turned dining room — with as many community, staff, homeless guests, and friends as we can fit in. (Long ago, William Morris, dreamer of new and old dreams, knew that the sacred spaces of churches should be places of community feasting.) It is a long time since our first Passover celebration in this house, getting in touch with the great symbols of freedom, of spring, of hope even in long oppression. Then, it will be Holy Week, and on Good Friday we plan to share a ritual that explores in song and reading, and litany and intercession the suffering of women, the most "despised and rejected" of those for whose liberation Jesus was prepared to endure a criminal's death. And on Easter eve, once more the house will be plunged in darkness as we wait to light the great candle from the new fire and carry it into the house to kindle small flames in every room and finally to the chapel once more, to share light, water, food, song and peace. It seems a long time since we began, hesitantly, and at first infrequently, to find ways to symbolize together the sources and meanings of our common life.

It began with a group of people deciding to share a home and open it to others in need. The experience of doing this challenged spiritual and theological growth and recognition, and recognition developed. The group of us was aware of itself simply as women and men reaching out to other women and men, people who were homeless, for that was the form of "need" that soon confronted us. The knowledge deepened and gradually also became more frightening and problematic as it became clearer. We confronted not just "homelessness" but radical dispossession, and mainly that of women.

Not all the poor are women, but when men are poor they experience what women experience all the time: they become people who have no ownership, but are owned. For women, laws may reluctantly change, but the old attitudes, the old realities, survive unchanged. Women are possessed and dispossessed, the ones who are wrong, the poor who are even poorer because their poverty is rendered invisible by being overlooked. So the recognition that grew for us was of women's homelessness — ours and theirs; the facts of the oppression of women, the exile of women, who make homes for the owners of the system but can never be secure or safe in them.

It was a long learning, and this book is about the learning, so it is partly story and partly reflection on the story. Some of it is funny, some of it is tragic, some of it is painful, some of it is joyful.

The setting is the old house which the original "Wellspring people" (who weren't yet called anything) found and bought in 1981. Its history should have warned us, but we only half recognized the meaning of it — the half we didn't recognize being that of the women who lived here, from 1649 until now. At first we learned about the house and its history as everyone else does, as a story of men, and it was and is part of that amazing (and usually ambiguous) story of the early settlers from England who spent months in tiny boats and began a new life in a place where everything had to be started over again — and often learned over again, since even the crops and the trees were different. And trees were what the house was built from.

When the people who became "Wellspring" bought the house they gradually discovered much of its history, partly from the formidable historical research which became necessary to establish title to the various parcels of land which went with it, and partly from a family descended from the original builders of the house. The settlers' name had been Eveleigh, one of those who came to New England with that same sense of seeking new land that had motivated the Wellspring group itself. The house was built in the style of many English houses of the time, a massive frame of oak sills and beams built around a great brick chimney. This house was somewhat larger than most; there were four main rooms, two up and two downstairs, each with its own hearth, and the rooms themselves were of good size, for the house served as an inn, even in those days, providing shelter "for man and beast". Like most country households of the time, it must also have been a farm with its own animals, bees, barns and fields, and the dairies and storage rooms needed to keep the household supplied with milk, cheese, honey, soap, and stores for grain and dried meat. There is still a bread oven built into the thickness of the chimney at the back of the great kitchen hearth, though that kitchen is now the living room of the house.

As a symbol of what the "Wellspring group" was about, and what it was to discover, the old building is powerful. The builders were, like ourselves, people with a vision, yet very practical. They dreamed of a "promised land" and set out to occupy it, and this included (as it had for the Hebrews) dispossessing the original inhabitants. Yet it *was* a magnificent and courageous enterprise.

This was a more prosperous household than many of the settlers' households. Sylvester Eveleigh built the house in 1649, it seems, or maybe it was his son John, and they prospered and were respected, and served as selectmen and did all the things good citizens should do. Sylvester served as a juryman, during the Salem witch trials. These were trials of women suspected of dealing with the powers of evil, because they knew more than most of their neighbors, or were more solitary, or owned things others coveted. There is no record of how Sylvester voted on that jury, or of how the women of his household felt in their secret thoughts about the trials and their fearful outcome.

There is no mention of the women in the recorded story of the house, apart from their names. Those names are familiar English ones — Bridget, (Sylvester's second wife), Mary, Sarah, Abigail. Their fathers, brothers and husbands bought land, built houses, farms and saw mills. They administered justice, which was greatly concerned with the ownership of land: the ownership of it, the disputes over it, the inheriting or disinheriting of it. Women were often part of the deal, as with Elizabeth Eveleigh who married a man called Rust, to whom the house passed in consequence. Women did not inherit land, unless there were no sons or if they were widows, and when they married, or remarried, the land passed to the husband.

Yet these women who lived in the house in the seventeenth century were a tough sisterhood. The older ones had come from England, leaving all they had ever known or loved of person or place, enduring the weary and dangerous months of the journey. They created a new life in a new, strange land and all of them lived lives of heavy labor in difficult conditions.

The room that was once the kitchen of the house — and also dining room, ale-room and general common space — is still a place to evoke wonder and sympathy in those who stand in it with imagination and compassion. It has a hearth nine feet wide, and customers and family sat around it; on it's fire women boiled and roasted and heated water. The huge original central beams and sills, the wide uneven oak floor boards, still enclose the household space, though other woodwork has been replaced. The door that kept out the weather and let in the people still does so — and lets in cold draughts too, as it has for three and a half hundred years. And the women who worked in that kitchen are still there in every brick.

These women were, then as now, landless and vulnerable, but they created the life in the land. They grew food and healing herbs, they cleaned, they made the clothes, they often dealt with all the financial details of the farms they could not own. They milked the cows and made butter and cheese, they salted and smoked meat for the winter, they ground the flour before the mills were built and they kneaded the dough and formed the loaves and baked them in the bread oven at the back of the hearth, where the fire never went out but, at night, was covered with ash and sods, ready to be uncovered and blown to a flame in the dawn.

They nursed the sick and the injured with skills handed down by other women, and decoctions from herbs they grew or found wild, helped by amulets, and by incantations whose words were already centuries old, women's songs of healing and prayer — to what god is not altogether clear.

Babies were brought to birth in the big bed in the room above the kitchen, while other women brewed herbal drinks to ease labor. While they waited for the birth they told tales — tales of the old country, stories of mother and grandmother, tales of fairies and witches, of kings and queens, of family and friends long left, of newer experiences — "Indians" and their ways and skills and customs, of neighbors, and of visitors from Boston or even from settlements in the far south.

In that room, also, they died, when the remedies failed, or in the fullness of years. Some died in childbirth, or of childbed fever. Babies died too, of the summer fever, or of the many childhood ailments. The women attended the deaths, too, with prayer and memories, with secret fears. Often enough they died, men and women, in the beds in which they were born and wed, for those who could afford to do so brought with them across the ocean the beds of their old homes, taken apart and corded in bundles. They hoped to renew the feather beds with feathers from new flocks of poultry.

The women strewed the bride-bed and the floor of the room with sweet herbs to expel evil spirits and bring good luck and many offspring, which were needed, seeing how fast the babies died. Marriage was what women were for, to provide sons to inherit the land. And then as now there were the other women, the servant girls who slept in the attic and were well- or ill-treated according to the mood of the master or mistress, and who were regarded as sexually available even in Puritan New England, and could not complain because it was always their fault anyway, and they might lose their jobs, which meant food and shelter, or be suspected of witchcraft for ensnaring a man.

Times change but this dynamic does not change much. In 1984, a girl of fifteen was admitted to a shelter. She was pregnant as a result of rape by her foster-father. The man, an upright citizen and church elder, and also his wife, blamed the girl for seducing him. The girl, like most women, accepted that it must have been her fault somehow, and refused to prosecute. The name of the game is still blaming the victim.

The house has a well in the front yard, and that was the reason for renaming it as we did. The name is descriptive but also symbolic. For a symbol to have meaning it must have a reference that really does evoke associations and feelings. "Wellspring" means, as a name, a source of life and growth, living water that keeps on welling up from the ground. The well also stands there, a reminder of how getting good water is hard work. Once, the women of the household turned the handle of the well pully and filled wooden buckets and carried them into the house, and the life of the house depended on that daily labor. Water to drink, water to cook with, water to wash the babies and the clothes and the pots, water for the cows, horses, pigs, and chickens which all households not right in town had to have.

Now the well stands unused, romantically covered with creepers that need to be cut back lest the well disappear altogether. (It did, one year, and ended up looking like a great bush.) The well is almost certainly polluted as well as unused, like so many other wells in this land where once everyone drew their water from them. That also is a tragic symbol, for together with the wells, many other sources of new life have been polluted and are no longer safe for living creatures. So the well for which the house is named is also a symbol of desire to discover unpolluted sources of life, for women and by women.

This house is full of women's stories; stories of courage and endurance, of comedy and tragedy, of heroism and betrayal, of silent misery and sudden rage, of friendship and compassion, of hope and despair. The men came in and went out, bound on errands in the big world, they were kind or they were unkind, tyrants or companions, just or brutal. They owned the land and the women. But the house is the gift of those women, their skill and hard work made it a place to live in. Though they had no ownership, they gave it life: white women and later black women, when a black freed slave called Freeman was given the house after the failure of a plantation in Ipswich. Nineteenth century photographs show their descendants, in pantalets and ringlets, stiff in Sunday-best clothes. Later still, the house was divided between two families, black and white. Once more, the men came and went, working the farm, earning, while the women kept the home. Did the black women and the white women become friends? Or did they live side by side in distrust and alienation?

The last of the Freemans was Hattie, whom older people in Gloucester still remember. With both families gone, the home empty around her and falling into disrepair, the wide oak floor boards buckling with damp and the roof leaking, Hattie clung to her home until she was too sick to care for herself. She refused to leave, and in the end had to be carried out. A photograph shows her as an old woman, standing in the doorway of the house, in her worn low-waisted dress of the twenties, her eyes smiling out.

Some time earlier, a young woman of one of the last of the white families to live in the house was courted by a young man at work on the new railroad line to Gloucester. Their great-granddaughter, Mary, died of leukemia at fifteen, eighteen months before the Wellspring story began; she smiles at us now from a photograph on the piano and another in the chapel, taken the day before she died, because Mary, who never saw it, is another of the women who have given life to this house.

Mary died before her full womanhood, yet in her encounter with death she broke open the full power of her maternity, nurturing other dying children in the hospital, exploring with her parents the great questions about loving, and grieving, and hoping. Her legacy to the Wellspring project was the deep compassion in her parents, which they shared with others also, and a certain relativizing of everyday problems and practicalities which they also shared, and which was important for the growth of a project most people regarded as highly impractical. Mary died eighteen months before the opening of Wellspring House, but only a few weeks after my own first meeting with some of those who later created Wellspring. She seemed to have a sense that she was able in the dying to leave a gift to the people in "her" parish, especially those who walked with her the last hard months and days, among whom were five of the original Wellspring group. And after her death, when the house was found but not yet bought, and nobody knew where the money was coming from, it seemed natural to entrust the project to Mary.

Mary died at the heart of a loving family, and did not grow up to confront consciously the hopes and the agonies of the other women whose stories are built into this house, but she was a woman, too, and her own ultimate struggle, her own victory over pain and fear, her own reaching out to the pain of others, her own faith in love stronger than death, are all at the heart of the Wellspring story. She remains a part of it all, a part of the word of God — the theology — to be heard here if one listens with care.

So Wellspring is a house drenched in the stories of women, old and new, women living in space belonging to others, their lives directed to the purposes of others. Now, the old house is a shelter for homeless families, almost all of them single mothers. They share it with the group which bought the house to make it into a home for people needing a place to heal. It has become a center of hope and a place of challenge. It is a home made by women, for women, but just because of that it is also a place where men and women, engage in the task of return from exile — their own exile. For the theme of the house and of the book is the fact of the exile of women, and with them of all that makes earth home for people, and the hope is that return from exile is possible, and the remaking of home for all people in our wounded earth.

The new story of Wellspring is about that fragile hope. This book is the story of a group of people who began to see a vision of homecoming, not all at once but in time and through shared experience. It grew out of a desire to share the events and experiences that went into the creation of a small source of help and hope for people without homes, and to show how that developed. In nine years the project grew from a low-profile attempt to live community life in a home open to people in need, to a well respected and effective program of sheltering, education and housing.

That, at least, is the public story. It is true, but there is another, inner story, which raises issues not only for those involved but for many. A result of this project has been both to find homes for many homeless people, and also to provide homes for some who would otherwise have become homeless. A result has also been to raise consciousness about homelessness, about housing, about the experiences of women on Welfare, about poverty. But a result also has been to change radically the living and thinking of the people who took part in the project.

So the Wellspring experience is about nine years of living in a house where homeless people can begin to put their lives back together and hope for a different future. It is about what happens to people who choose to live there, as well as those who are obliged to live there. What kind of people they are, why they are there, and what the experience *does* to them. And it is about the questions they raise, and that we raise around them. This is doing what people of faith have always had to do, trying to make sense of belief, vocation, salvation, sin, and all the religious issues—in terms of their own time and place, their own fears and prejudices and learned responses. It is perhaps a theology of women in our society, in our land — or rather, as we discovered, of women in exile from the land.

If this book is part story, part reflection, part rage, part question and part dream, it seems to me that this is actually not an unusual way of dealing with reality. First you experience it, then you ask questions. What was going on? How did it all begin? Why did it happen? To live at all, we constantly process our experiences, sometimes honestly and appropriately, sometimes with rationalization, needing to blame others for what went wrong, take credit for what went right. Or if there is no convenient human scapegoat, and no way we can feel in control, then God comes in very handy, or some other kind of household deity. Whether it was bad luck, good luck, God's will, the stars or the zodiac, there are interpretations, stored up for us by generations before us, or learned from friends. One way or another we interpret experiences, and then the interpretation comes into play the next time we deal with similar experience.

That is why this book is both story and theology. In fact, theology is reflection on the human story, an attempt to interpret experiences in order to understand the operation of divine presence and energy in created existence. But that means we have to do theology as best we can through a mix of learned cultural attitudes and expectations. If our culture deeply believes that women are inevitably sensual and seductive creatures we base our domestic attitudes and our legal codes on that, and our moral theology will reflect that conviction too, and in its turn it will underpin and justify the domestic and legal subjection of women for their own good, their almost literal "dispossession". When that gets changed we find ourselves changing the theology and spirituality as well. Was it the spirituality and the theology that became questionable in the light of renewed awareness of the gospel? Or did we begin to reread the gospels because we were questioning the old theology, or because we were revolting against the old experience? Which comes first, the chicken or the egg?

The important thing about this progression is that it relativizes theological statements and spiritual categories.

This doesn't mean that we simply discard the religious insights of the past and begin again. We need to understand how previous generations came to formulate their theology, *why* they needed the kind of spiritual descriptions they lived by. That helps us not to absolutize our own insights; for ourselves, too, we need to understand the "why" and "how" of our theologies.

But the "whys" and "hows" are not purely intellectual. The drive to discover a new way to describe and act comes out of *feeling*. Fear impelled the witch hunts of the past as it impels the gang rapes of the present, and both produce their own elaborate justifications among those who practice them. A rage of compassion impelled the mission of Jesus and shaped his theology of God and his attitude to oppressor and oppressed. A rage of just anger bred the theology of liberation from people finally perceiving that the oppression they had suffered for generations was not inevitable, or God's will, but a reversible decision of greedy power-holders. Theology grows even from what seems to be very narrow and limited experiences, as women's experiences have usually been.

I am a white, educated woman, though not academic. (I used to wish I had been academic but now I'm not sure. The academic world, so deeply attractive to the scholar and thinker in me, seems to be ineradicably structured by patriarchs.) I do not and cannot cry with the voice of those who have most suffered dispossession. Yet, as a woman, I know the marks of even a comfortable exile, I know what it means to lack ownership, in myself and as I perceive it in women around me. So I write as a middle-class white woman whose tradition is Catholic, and therefore I reach a readership mostly Catholic and middle-class and white. My interpretation stems from that — these are my limitations but also my riches.

Hundreds of years ago, there lived a woman in England who was, as far as we can tell, middle-class, and certainly literate. We do not even know her name, for she came to be called after the church against whose walls she had decided to live, in a two-room hermitage. The church was the Church of St. Julian and we know her as Dame Julian of Norwich. Within her lifetime she experienced the "Black

Death" — the plague that killed half the population of the country. It came three times — once when she was a young 'teenager, once in her early twenties and once in her late twenties. Half the population died. She saw men, women, and children die in fever and pain, peasants, priests, nobles, nuns, beggars, bakers, weavers, sailors, housewives, babies. It seemed as if death were the whole of reality — the sight of it, the smell of it, the sound of it. Certainly, members of her family must have died, though she never mentioned it in her writing.

Soon after, this woman became ill herself, and seemed about to die — indeed she had prayed to experience this, in order to understand in her own body the deathly woe which Christ had suffered. In this way, perhaps, she could make sense of what she had experienced. In her lifetime, too, she had witnessed the peasants' revolt, when half-starved men rebelled against the oppressive brutality of nobles and churchmen. Their rage erupted in random violence, they broke open the prisons and let out the poor imprisoned there — but among them the murderers and robbers. They killed those whom they perceived as their persecutors, but finally were defeated by the king's false promises and their leaders were hideously punished.

All this, as well as the routine brutality of life, Julian saw and felt and pondered. Yet she never wrote of it directly. Instead, in her agony of sickness in which she struggled with the fearful and physical power of evil itself, she perceived the wounded and dying Christ, and later wrote down what had been shown to her. What she developed in long years of reflection was unexpected, for it was an account of a God who cannot hate, cannot punish, a God who is mother, a Christ whose divinity consists in a capacity for tender and nurturing motherhood. "So how can anything be amiss?" This was not the escapism of a person unable to deal with evil. This was the fruit of a willingness to move into, and beyond, brutality and destruction and fear and death, and to discover a reality encompassing it all, a spring of joy and hope and healing in the most atrocious circumstances. The theology of the motherhood of God — the God who gives birth, who embraces and gives food, who weeps because of suffering and desires healing and comfort — this was the fruit of long years of wrestling with real events and people and feelings. Julian's interpretation came out of her limited experience, but it's profundity was a gift that has been rediscovered in a time of great need, by people with very different experiences.

The Wellspring experience is limited, my experience is limited. It is what we have, and it is what we can share, it is how we do theology — theology out of women's experience at a particular time and place, yet perhaps not limited to that time and place only.

"Liberation" theology of a particular kind is at the basis of the Wellspring story which I am about to tell, but not because the Wellspring people embraced it and decided to apply its insights. It *became* a theology Wellspring had to have because of the emotional charge produced by the experience, the urgent need to discover a meaning and a process to make sense of the suffering of the women who came to us. So to reflect on the emergence of that theology has been helpful for us, as for many others. Yet what we have here is not simply a theology we decided to adopt because it was there and more or less fit. We encountered what is called "liberation theology" and it helped to make sense of our experience, but the experience changed this theology too, and pushed and shaped it into something new, and what is still growing is not just one more "system" but a way of asking questions and living them — questions about women, and land, and prophecy, and God, or Goddess.

Why did some kind of "liberation theology" emerge when it did? What was it that made it impossible for poor people any longer to believe that their lot was a God-given trial to prepare them for a blessed eternity? Was it Marxist literature that began to influence people? Or did socialist ideas begin to make sense because reading the gospels in one's own language undermined the accepted spirituality of patient acceptance? Or did groups begin to read Scripture because they had already lost confidence in the old way of religion?

How do people begin to name themselves as oppressed? Where and when do the cracks first appear? What causes the cracks? How are they identified as cracks that could be widened? What is the mysterious gestation of revolution? These are questions raised wherever people are changing. The Wellspring experience is not that of Haiti, or El Salvador, or Afghanistan, or Peru or Poland or West Virginia or Brixton or Northern Ireland or the inner city of Chicago or Jobstown, near Dublin, or the mining villages of Yorkshire or any of the million places on this small planet where there are people struggling with oppression and trying to change it. Wellspring is small and undramatic compared with some of these, yet the dramas of lives caught up in this struggle are epic. The stage is small, but the women are universal, they reach from earth to heaven. They themselves do theology this way (not knowing it), reflecting on their concrete experiences as particular people. Wellspring is the laboratory at work, rather than the published conclusions.

An analogy may help. In York, in England, there is a permanent exhibit called "Jorvik", which initiates the visitor into the daily lives of Viking settlers who lived on that exact spot eleven hundred years ago. Years of digging and careful research have made possible the recreation of a Viking village, not only with its people and buildings but its sounds and smells.

But besides taking the visitors through this re-constructed village, the tour continues through a section of the "dig" itself, where the cut-through, labelled, layers of soil shows where and how the remains were discovered which made the reconstruction possible. And finally there is the laboratory itself, itself reconstructed to show how, and with what tools and techniques, the researchers examined their finds and drew their conclusions. Thus the visitor learns not only what the conclusions about Viking life are (as shown in the recreated village) but what were the data from which those conclusions were drawn and also how they were reached. But, importantly, the experience comes first, the sights, sounds, smells and the *feelings* excited by all this.

This book does the same thing. It takes a complex lived experience and describes some of it, it tries to give the reader a sense of the "sources", the material used for theological reflection. It displays the tools and techniques used to understand what is going on, so that their validity can be judged, but it also puts the reader in touch with the feelings. And it reaches some conclusions, theological conclusions which, in many ways, do not agree with some older ones. They are different because the premises are different, and the premises themselves are different because the experiences make the old premises untenable. I do not mean only the immediate experiences described, but the worldwide experiences of disruption, doubt and fear which have undermined confidence in the old power structures and their moral, theological and ideological underpinnings. The cracks appear, but instead of assuming that cracks in the fortress walls are just waiting for the repair crew, we recognize them as opportunities, as signs of possible liberation. If there are cracks, the wall might be vulnerable after all. Maybe a little judicious use of the crowbar will help things along.

So the way this book is put together is dictated by its aim. It explores the implications of the experience of being with homeless women, how it all began and how the feeling and the thinking changed and where we sought for symbols and interpretations (as Julian did in her time). It notices how the experience changed people and wonders why and what for, and faces some of the more disturbing results of allowing oneself to change, and comes to some more theological conclusions. It goes further and recovers the rage that was converting, that closed the doors to the comfortable past and made hospitality a political issue. In considering the need for change it explores the way God is used to prevent it, for the will of a God who likes people passive is most convenient for those who fear the anger of the poor.

But anger is not enough. Grieving becomes essential if we are to recognize evil and know what had been done and thus be able to experience newness and so the story is about women grieving, the necessity of it, and the prophetic power of it. And all this is part of the preparation for a long journey home from exile, to reclaim and rebuild the homeland that others have controlled and exploited and almost destroyed.

If this is a story, there is a story teller — myself. I am also a character in the story, so that it seems inevitable that it is written quite frankly in a directly personal way. This is my way of telling the story, these are my perceptions and interpretations and my conclusions. All the characters in the story are real, and are known to many. For that reason, also inevitably, some things are not told. There are stories within all stories, and not all of them need to or can be told, and no apology for that is required. Likewise, the names of some of the guests at Wellspring, whose lives are stories within the story, are changed here, and even details altered a little, because some aspects of their pain and their struggle should not be made public. They will identify themselves if they read this, but they have a right to privacy in essentials. The whole story, all the stories, cannot be told except in the intimate sharing of close friends. Enough is told here, I hope, to put readers in touch with an experience which raises issues — theological, spiritual, political — that people of faith (any faith, religious or not) need to confront, and soon. The Wellspring experience is one of struggle, hope, discouragement and renewed hope and struggle. The story does not end, because the work does not end until injustice and oppression end and the exiles return to their homeland "carrying their sheaves". Meanwhile, this story and this search for meaning are not only a tale, they are a celebration, a song like the long tales sung by the fireside in gatherings of friends and neighbors. When the people of Israel were exiled to Babylon, the people there asked the exiles to sing them songs of their far off country, and they found it hard to do so in alien surroundings. "How can I sing the song of Yahweh in a strange land?" Yet it was, in the end, very important to do so, for that singing recalled the place that is home, makes it once more real. Singing breaks down walls of apathy and depression. Singing is essential if change is to come, it is the beginning of liberation. It helps hearts open to anger and to grief and also to hope. So it matters that we sing our songs of home in this strange land. This is one of them.

CHAPTER ONE
HOMELESS WOMEN

Wellspring House takes in women who are homeless in the sense that they literally have no other place to go. Some have been sleeping in cars, some have been sharing with families or friends, who cannot keep them any longer because of overcrowding or who simply throw them out. Some are evicted because they cannot pay the rent (maybe it suddenly went up, or a husband and his earnings disappeared, or she lost a job); some are evicted because the property is bought for redevelopment; some leave home because of abuse. Often there is a combination of these things — for instance, a woman leaves home because of abuse and moves in with her mother, who soon tells her to leave, so she sleeps in her car.

These women, and their children, are obviously homeless, but there is a sense in which their homelessness began long before it reached the point at which they literally had no shelter. There is a sense in which all women, with a few exceptions, are "homeless", even if they live in comfortable homes, because they belong to the sex that does not possess, that is, on the contrary, possessed.

The police brought a young woman to Wellspring about midnight. She had been beaten by her boyfriend and needed a safe place for the night. It turned out that the boyfriend, who was drunk, had beaten her in her own apartment, for which she paid the rent, and had then fallen asleep on her couch. She called the police because she was afraid of what might happen when he woke, and their response was to remove her (to Wellspring) and leave *him* on the couch. They did not remove him, even though it was her apartment. This is a good example of how our society feels about women and property. The police in this case were kind and concerned — it just did not occur to them to regard her as the owner of that space, with the right to inhabit it unmolested. It is *the women who leave.* Courts grant restraining orders which are supposed to bar a violent man from access to the house after violence, but restraining orders are notoriously hard to enforce because the police won't come unless he actually tries to break in, or does break in, by which time it's probably too late. Most people — often including the abused women — feel that the man has a right to be there. When there is violence, few women call the police to have the man removed, because they know the police probably will not do so. In one local case the reaction of a policeman to a woman with a bloody nose, cut cheeks and black eye, was "he has a right to do what he likes in his own home"! Many police are, in contrast, compassionate people who try to help, but they, and the women themselves, are up against a basic feeling that the house belongs to the man (never mind who pays the rent) and if the woman can't take his behavior, *she* should leave. And she does.

One woman, interviewed after she applied to come to Wellspring, explained that she and her husband had together built a house and paid for it. He "was tired of being married" and turned her out with their two children. Asked if she might go to court to get her half-share of the property, she responded that her husband had said to her, "You wouldn't take my home away from me, would you?" This pathetic plea seemed to her to end the matter.

Even when there is no obvious violence, even when the relationship is regarded as "normal", the same underlying assumption holds: the house, the land, the nation, belongs to the men. Women are there to support the men, and are valued and even loved when they do so well and faithfully.

This is the description of the role of the traditional wife — she exists to create a good environment for her man and his children. The famous description of a good woman in the Book of Proverbs, who manages her household, a farm, and even runs a business, indicates that she does all this so that her husband may feel secure and earn the respect of his neighbors. Her existence, however much loved and praised, is justified because it serves his interests and those of her sons. Many women accept this role and feel comfortable in it because it gives them a sense of being valued. One of the reasons why the women's movement only became a real power in the nineteenth century, and still does not appeal to all women, is that many middle and upper class women, and even peasant wives, had, as those solely responsible for often large households and possessions, a satisfying degree of responsibility, a career involving many skills which were appreciated and gave real power and a sense of fulfillment. It enabled many women to tolerate a high degree of marital alienation and even abuse. Yet however well it can work for many women the whole situation is based on the fact that women have no ownership. They lack ownership of themselves. They are radically homeless, they are dependent for place, for identity, for purpose, on another, be he father, husband, "lover", boss, priest, or God-image.

In 1836 Caroline Norton experienced what the legal "homelessness" of women meant and refused to accept it. Locked in a marriage in which her husband had beaten and abused her every since their honeymoon, she had three sons, and wrote novels and poems which earned the family income her lazy husband would not provide. Yet when, after a particularly painful fight, she took refuge temporarily with a friend, she found on returning that she was locked out of her home and denied access to her children. Against the advice of all she knew, who counseled submission and "discretion", she decided to fight. It took many years, for she discovered that she had no legal rights at all — to her home, to her children, even to her own earnings, which automatically belonged to her husband. She was also automatically suspect — she *must* be a "bad" woman for such a situation to arise. The story of her persistence, of her suffering, (and of the suffering of her children, who were neglected by the father who refused to allow their mother to see them) is only one of many such stories of heroism. Caroline did find some support — in the end some changes were made in the law. After another one hundred and fifty years a woman, now, in many countries, has equal rights in law to custody of her children, to the home, and a full right to her earnings. Yet, as the story told above demonstrates, the underlying assumptions have not changed very much.

Actual physical homelessness, then, merely makes obvious what is already inherent in the position of women. To understand this, it is essential to realize that this applies to many poor men also. The actual homelessness of *any* person is the expression of society's judgement that they lack humanity. Once a person has failed to hold onto property in the form of a job, or enough money to own or rent a place to live, that person is treated differently. That person is totally dependent on others' decisions, even whims. Men who have had the experience of sudden poverty have told about what happens to their attitudes and feelings. Such a man must learn to accept rudeness, must wait in line, must be grateful; he must become responsive to the moods of those who hold the power, because they can save or damn him. Self-image changes quickly, his behavior becomes servile, he has to be content with little, he learns to suppress rage or protest because the expression of such feelings could forfeit the favors of the possessor. Soon he no longer even feels them — he internalizes his subjection.

I have purposely used the masculine pronoun here, because this makes it very clear that homelessness is, basically, a social judgement on a person. And all that is said above of the person who loses property is true at all times of women, unless and until they decide to change — themselves, and the situation. Meanwhile, inevitably, because women have no "rights" in the full sense, they are subject to violence. They are still spiritually "property", no matter what changes in the law have been made, and men who abuse women are simply acting out of this deep cultural conviction. If one's property proves inadequate one is justified in a response of anger and blame and, if necessary, punishment. This is the link between homelessness and violence against women: the homeless are non-owners, dependent possessions, and women are essentially homeless (until they take the difficult road to recovered self-ownership) therefore women are subject to punishment if they do not fulfill their one purpose: to satisfy the demands of a male, and of a male dominated society.

We need to remind ourselves of what can happen to whole peoples if they are dispossessed — homeless — and dependent on the chancy goodwill of the possessor for somewhere to live, for survival. The Jewish people, driven from their homeland, were for many centuries homeless, settling where they could, or were allowed. Because they were not possessors they were the "others", different and suspect. The ways in which they tried to preserve their identity and hope, their customs, rituals, language, marked them as peculiar, possibly evil. (Women experience this too. The traditional lore of women, the ways of coping handed down from mother to daughter, the spells for a good husband, the jokes, the companionship, the concerns and feelings men do not share — these become proof that women are unreliable, irrational, tricky. The solidarity of women becomes a threat.)

When misfortune struck a community, or personal disaster fell on an individual, the Jewish community was the obvious scapegoat. Centuries of persecution, justified as punishment for their crimes as "Christkillers" and bolstered by stories of human sacrifice, culminated in the Holocaust, when millions of Jews, the "others", the natural scapegoats for Germany's misfortunes, were hideously slaughtered.

With the Jews to the gas chambers went gypsies, the archetypal dispossessed, outcasts in every land, suspected of everything from chicken stealing to kidnapping of children, hunted, imprisoned, hanged. This is what happens to those who are homeless, who have no claim to the land on which they are suffered to live.

This is, clearly enough, a condition of slavery. The African people, kidnapped, transported to be sold as plantation slaves, and their descendants, were homeless in the most obvious sense. They lived on someone else's land, under conditions over which they had no control. They had no rights at all.

But at least in more recent times the one thing that made spiritual survival possible for these dispossessed people in the face of persecution — their sense of solidarity and identity as a people — has been denied to women. In some tribal societies women may be inferior but they have their own sisterhood, their rituals and customs, which bind them together and give them self-respect. In western society women's rituals and gatherings were — not too long ago — proof of witchcraft. These gatherings were, indeed, survivals of long ago women's rituals of worship, proscribed when Europe became Christian. They are still proscribed though more subtly — by mockery and triviliazing of anything women do together. Women in western society were and are expected to find their identity in the male-centered family, first their father's, then their husband's. Isolated from each other except for social gatherings, they internalize a male view of women, and know no other. This is why it is hard for most women to question their state of dispossession. They have no "ground" from which to view it. Dispossession is inside them.

In the United States, and also in Britain, and other ex-colonial countries, the black people are among the dispossessed, with fewer well-paid jobs, less land, lower incomcs and less education, than other poor people. And black women are the poor even among poor women. This book, written by a white woman out of experience mainly with white women, cannot presume to speak for black women, but when we reflect on the dispossession of women we are feeling our way into a way of being, at deeper and even unconscious levels, which probably only the descendants of slaves can fully understand. For this very reason, perhaps, it is the writings of black women which have helped to open the eyes of white women to the realities of womankind. (It was not only black women who learned to understand themselves better because they read — or saw the movie of — Alice Walker's "The Color Purple"!)

The experience of powerlessness, of dependence on another not only for home and food but for identity and role, means that women blame themselves when things go wrong. Since a woman's role is to make a man happy, if he isn't happy she must have failed. This has been drilled into girls from childhood, by parents, by magazines, by all the men they meet. If the man goes with other women, if he drinks, if he beats her, that must be because she has failed. She blames herself, and he blames her, and so does his mother, her father, the police — even, often enough, the judge to whom she may finally resort for help as violence increases.

One woman came to Wellspring with her baby to escape an abusive relationship. She was angry and swore she would never see the man again, but within days she was going out with him. One night one of the staff at Wellspring was called out by a friend of this woman, to try to calm her down. She had had a verbal fight with the man and later was drinking. She said she wanted to go and find him again. In spite of all persuasion she insisted on going after him, and found him in a barroom; he insulted her and knocked her down. Next day she excused him, "because I asked for it." It is very hard for women to be truly convinced that *nobody* deserves to be treated like that, no matter what they have done.

Mary Kay, one of the women who took part in a mission training program developed by Wellspring in its early years, to help Christians prepare to serve need in their own country, did part of her two-year field work in a shelter for abused women in West Virginia. (This mission program was significant for Wellspring and for this book and I will return to it.) The Appalachian regional culture accepts wife-beating as normal, and the fundamentalist religion re-enforces this, teaching women to be submissive and obedient and to accept whatever treatment their husbands mete out, as their God-sent lot in life. A woman who has finally reached the limit of submissiveness, often after years of abuse, may be driven by sheer terror for her life to take refuge. Yet, over and over, these women will say, "I know I deserved it, I burned the dinner," or "I answered him back, so I guess I deserved it."

In a different milieu, a middle-class woman was regularly beaten by her husband as an accompaniment to his sexual demands, which were made three or four times a day. Only after ten years did she finally leave, explaining to friends, "I thought maybe marriage was like that, and I'd chosen it, so I thought I should stay."

An elderly woman, who finally came to Wellspring, had suffered forty years of physical, sexual and emotional abuse. Several times she left home, but the Minister of her church, her doctor, as well as "friends", urged her to go back. The Minister preached the sanctity of marriage, the doctor felt her injuries were "not so terrible", friends were sure "he'll be different now!" Another elderly woman, after twelve years of abuse, including sexual abuse, came to us with a broken wrist which is permanently weakened, and other injuries. Her husband would not allow her to leave home except to go to church, so she finally arrived at Wellspring with nothing but a Bible in one hand and a purse in the other.

Individual stories are harrowing, and Wellspring hears many, but telling them can sometimes give the impression that we are talking about terrible but exceptional cases. Here are some figures. These are conservative figures, based on available hard evidence; much violence is never reported because women are afraid of more punishment if they speak:

In the United States between two and four thousand women die each year as a direct result of battering. *(FBI statistics.)*

Abuse of women happens in about half of all male/female cohabiting relationships. *(National Clearinghouse on Domestic Violence.)*

One out of seven women is a victim of marital rape. *(From "Rape in Marriage by Diana Russell)*

In a smaller survey done by the Connecticut Task Force on abused women it was established that, of 274 women interviewed, 45% had been kicked, beaten, otherwise abused by their husbands, 29% reported they were beaten with weapons and suffered broken bones, and 40% said their children had also been beaten by their husbands.

The final chilling statistic put together from available sources shows that in the U.S.A. a woman is beaten by her husband *every eighteen seconds.* So we are not talking about something exceptional. We are talking about an endemic attitude of fear and hatred towards women. The statistics naturally do not attempt to include the emotional violence, everything from recurrent violent rage and verbal abuse to the decades-long accumulation of denigrating and humiliating words and behavior which destroy self-respect and hope. It is true that the urge to violence towards women is often kept under control by civilized habits and in some cases actually eliminated by the effects of a caring family, but this saving reality is always at odds with the public denigration and contempt for women shown on every billboard, movie theatre poster, or magazine.

The overall picture is one of almost unquestioned violence against women, whether physical or emotional, which most men either commit or condone, and which is condoned by many (maybe most) women also, because they, too, deeply believe that if women are abused it is because they have done wrong, or at least *are* wrong: ugly, incompetent, too independent, etc. etc. As one woman said, explaining why her husband drove her from their home, (which both had worked to pay for) "He said I'm too fat." So the cycle continues; mothers teach their daughters that this is how it is, this is what women are for and may expect. If they can't keep a man happy, (their father, their brother, their boss, their boyfriend or husband) then they've got it coming to them. Most women will sympathize with each other but they will not expect, or even really want, any change.

The basic reason why many do not deeply "want" to change the pattern of oppression is that they believe that they themselves are bad. It is a despair so deep that many are not fully aware of it, although it affects all their attitudes, actions and decisions. Over the years at Wellspring we gradually became aware of one of the reasons for this: incest is a statement that women are a possession — a body to use, whose needs are irrelevant. The female body — whether it be that of a baby or a 'teenage girl — is not a person, because this female thing has no rights, no ownership. It is to be owned and used, and most perpetrators of incest are convinced they have a perfect right to do what they do.

There are support groups for women at Wellspring once or twice a week. They are for women in the house, for women who have left and like to come back for that, and for other women locally. In one early group of about ten, when the women began sharing their stories, they realized that every woman but one in the group was a survivor of incest. These were not all "poor" women. There were some from comfortable homes, educated professional women, working at Wellspring as volunteers. Recently, Nancy and I were asked to speak to a class at a University which was studying feminist theology. The room was packed with young men and women, affluent, at least from professional homes. We spoke of the statistics of abuse, the experience of incest and what it does to people. The silence was total. Some heads dropped, some stared ahead, fighting tears. Afterwards the woman teaching the class confirmed that she knew directly or indirectly that many in the class were survivors of incest. A few came up and said so. One wonders how many never told at all.

Over the years we at Wellspring have learned to "listen" for the signs that somewhere in the past of a guest in the house the incest experience is half-buried, denied, but operative. Over and over again, when a level of trust has been established, truth is admitted, with shame, with a kind of apology at first. Then the tears follow, and the helpless rage flows, the screaming against those who have done this to them.

Statistics collected by Children's Hospital Medical Center (Massachusetts) shows that in the U.S.A. by the age of eighteen 25% of all girls and 10% of all boys will have experienced sexual abuse, and in 80% to 90% of cases the perpetrators are male family members. Once more, we are not talking of terrible exceptions, we are talking about something that happens in homes at all economic and social levels.

The severity of the experience varies. It may be a "one time" incident, and if a parent or older friend is available to listen, to affirm "it wasn't your fault", even to go through the process of confrontation of the perpatrator, the child may emerge with little permanent damage. But even when the experience happens "only once" it can destroy a life. One woman came to Wellspring from a drug re-hab program. She was 27, and had been into drugs and prostitution since the age of fourteen. At age eleven she was raped by a close family friend in the presence of her brothers. She went to her mother, weeping and bleeding, was locked in her room and told she was a whore. Her father, to whom she had always been the "little princess' who could do no wrong, refused to speak to her ever again. She was sent to a school for "bad" girls (her description) and there followed a history of truancy punished by more severe penalties until she took to the streets and began to live out the label which had been put on her, covering the pain with more and more drugs. She was in and out of rehab programs, married (a drug dealer) and had a child who was born heroin-addicted and fostered. Tremendous ego-strength and intelligence enabled her to survive. Even now, battling with AIDS, she lives and hopes to change. Her family are all racketeers and drug dealers, but she is the one who is "bad".

In some cases, however, incest may continue for years, and the child may be afraid to tell anyone, or may really believe it when the perpetrator tells her "there's no harm in it, it's just our secret, but we won't tell Mommy because she wouldn't understand." Often, indeed, the mother will condone or even encourage incest with her daughter or daughters as a way of avoiding unwelcome sex herself. Some children are involved in incestuous relationships from early childhood into adolescence, trapped in a net of fear and guilt, bribed and threatened to keep quiet. Some are kept silent by the deep shame of the fact that the experience is pleasurable, for incest is not always violent. The pleasure is not so much sexual, rather there can be an element of welcome intimacy and physical closeness that a child craves, especially if, as is sometimes the case, the mother is unloving. So the aftermath is even more guilt-ridden and hard to admit.

What incest does to a person is to destroy their sense of identity and their sense of limits. Who am I, if my father is my lover, and if my mother is my rival — or procuress? Who am I, in the high school years of dating, if I am already sexually experienced in a way I can't admit? And what are the limits, if a person I need and trust can so betray me, if father, uncle, brother, can use me, if my mother and others refuse to believe me, or encourage the incest (sometimes, incredibly, *both*)? We see the signs many times — the inability to be "real" about options, (because what is "real"?) the tendency to live in one fantasy after another (because real life is *not* real), the flight from one man to another, (because who can I trust, and who would really want a person like me?) The self-blame, the *choosing* of ways that will be destructive or painful, are ways in which survivors of incest punish themselves for their "sin". Often they dare not be angry with the perpetrator, who is the parent, or parent-figure, and whom there is therefore a deep need to justify so that one may love him. So the anger is directed against one's self, but it is not understood or acknowledged and, often, one of the signs of the incest experience is an obscure depression with no assignable cause. Depression is suppressed anger. It seeks to punish the person who feels it. (I'm no good, I'm evil, there must be something bad in me for this to have happened.) And it isolates, because telling is forbidden. Who could accept me if they knew?.

Once, Wellspring hosted a course in counseling for cases of rape and incest. The course was given by a Rape and Incest Center team, and the Wellspring staff were there, with a few people from outside. One of the group at the time was a young woman who was herself a survivor of incest. As the chilling statistics were detailed, as we learned a little of the effects of sexual abuse, of the legal remedies and the process of helping rape victims, of ways to help incest survivors to find a way forward, this young woman became almost rigid with remembered anger. She had told her story long before, had, she thought "put it behind her." She had been determined to repair the broken family ties, to re-create family bonding, to live a new life as if the incest had never been. It took some courage to attend the course, and she did it, yet no matter what was said of the long-term effects of incest, of the need to be in touch with the experience and work through it, that was for other people. She herself could only continue to live as if the past had not been, as if the condoning mother were indeed the good parent she longed for. But the anger was still there, displaced onto those she loved, still threatening her achievement of stability.

If I seem to dwell on this widespread evil I do so because this, too, helps us to recognize that the root of the evil is not incest, itself, or the violence against women and children, but the deep fear of women which pervades our society. Or rather it is a fear of the feminine, a fear of the potential "traitor within", the intuitive wisdom and imagination, the compassion and the bodiliness, that, if given its freedom threatens to undermine the vast superstructure of masculine power. This power claims dominance and control over everything, the right to order creation, and human lives, to its own self-created purposes. It has immense skill, knowledge and power, it thinks it has the whole world (and space) in its hands — almost. But this divine conviction cannot endure the questioning, the undermining influence, of the feminine powers in each one, man or woman. The voices of the poor, the very existence of the weak, the presence of mystery, or of deep personal feeling, bring in question the absolute control, the absolute rightness. If the "others" can be discredited or suppressed, all may yet be well.

The trouble is, women embody all this — the lack of physical power combined with the mysterious power to give life, the claims to feelings, to intuitive awareness and compassion, the courage and strength which seem to have different values and different goals. If men, as conditioned as women by a society which enslaves them in one-sided masculinity, are to survive they cannot tolerate this attack on their sense of having it all under control.

Nobody knows if the incidence of incest and abuse against women has increased over recent years, because there are no statistics for earlier periods. But there is evidence that in countries where male dominance is less threatened by women than in the U.S.A. the rates are lower. These are cultures where women are less apt to question their role of submissive supporter, therefore the suppression of women is done culturally and politically with little fuss. (This does not mean that there is no violence against women in such cultures, but it is more likely to be directed against women who "sin", i.e. who do not accept their role.)

But in the U.S. and some other western countries women have become, publicly, less submissive. They can compete for male jobs, they have legal rights, they make demands. The cultural pressure for submission and silence is still very strong, as we have seen, but the *sanctions* against "uppity women" are no longer operated by law and public custom in the same way. It may be, therefore, that there *is* more domestic violence and incest, because both of these are basically assertions of power, attempts to force the women (and indirectly the feminine within) into submission and powerlessness, and to punish her for implicitly questioning the sole possession of the male. (Recent figures — 1988 — for homicides show that there has been a sharp increase in the number of women killed by men since the legal protection available to abused women has increased.)

Wherever men are themselves subjected to humiliation, when their jobs are threatened or their personal dignity assailed (by an unjust boss, by "the law", or simply by ill-fortune) the level of domestic violence rises. Social workers are well aware of this. This is not a phenomenon of poverty only. Men in highly paid professional jobs — architects, politicians, doctors, therapists, directors of businesses, as well as lesser beings — also experience humiliation, fear of loss of dignity or power, with the same result. Sometimes education can re-impose the taboos of civilization, and reduce physical abuse, but emotional abuse can be even more insidiously destructive of self-respect and hope. The wounded male ego, trained by the culture to value itself by its ability to earn, control, and dominate, vents its anger and misery on the available scapegoats — the ones who, by their own vulnerability, powerfully symbolize and irritate the sense of being weak which our society disallows. It is appropriate, right and satisfying, therefore, to punish them for being weak. It gives a sense of restored power, because, in our culture, the definition of power is the ability to dominate others, and to hurt them or be kind to them as one thinks fit. The "punishment" is not always direct abuse. Going with other women, withholding or gambling away money, or simply disappearing, are effective ways of inflicting punishment. The results are equally to reinforce the guilt and self-blame of the women.

This is what I have learned in nine years at Wellspring. This is what all of us have talked about, researched about, prayed about. We tell each other that what we are about is "the empowerment of women." We must be saying that we hope to find a way to break out of this horrible circle of guilt, and despair. What a thing to undertake! Are we to heal a whole sick culture? There's no doubt it's a good thing to help a few women find new homes and begin again. But somehow or other we implicitly committed ourselves to something more. We talk about gospel values, about change, a different possibility.

Social workers, counselors, doctors — they find themselves becoming anxious and irritable, losing their temper with those they are trying to help, beginning to drink more, blaming their families, leaving jobs unfinished. They feel perpetually angry, finally they quit, or else settle into a cynical minimum of work to keep the money coming, closing out the suffering they cannot alleviate and can no longer face. Sometimes they break down and are sick for long periods. This is "burn-out".

We have felt the signs of burn-out ourselves: the irritation at the behavior of homeless guests, the annoyance at each other, the "heaviness" at staff meetings, the enormous fatigue which is emotional as well as physical and mental. After all we live with our job. Some of us live in the house with the guests, all of us eat with them, spend all day with them. So it never goes away. Sometimes we wish it would — or we feel *we* will. A weekend break or a celebration relieves the feeling. Someone goes away on vacation, and comes back full of new ideas and experiences and hopes, and things look better. But none of this goes to the root.

How can we be about empowerment when we understand that this does not mean merely helping a few women to get out of the abyss of poverty, but also means addressing the things that keep them poor — inwardly and outwardly oppressed. And how is the basic alienation of women related to the alienation of our whole society? What *is* so wrong that the effects are those I have described?

What is wrong is a condition of slavery, and of exile — both these things.

Slavery means being totally subject to the needs and demands of someone else.

Exile means having no claim to the land you live in, even if you were born there. It means being a permanent alien.

The two things generally go together, and the realization of the meaning of these two human experiences provides a basis for understanding the situation of women, of our society, of our earth, and perhaps a way to change them. The realization of meaning breaks through in the discovery of two great symbols of Jewish history and identity which Christians have inherited: the Exodus experience of liberation from slavery and the Exile experience leading to return and rebuilding.

This discovery came not by reading and reflecting but by celebrating.

The Wellspring group is a faith community with varied backgrounds but a common motivation and a common need to express that motivation in ritual. At first people just went to church, but the nature of the work and the life quickly exposed the unreality in much of what passes for worship, at least for us. We began "doubling" — if some still went to church we wanted also to do something that could express for us, as a group, the meaning of at least the great celebrations.

So, tentatively, and even with fear, we began to shape our own rituals — for Christmas, for Holy Week. Later, driven by internal need, we developed a weekly celebration. So we read Scripture, but also contemporary readings that reflect the same themes. Likewise, the music we choose (whether on tape or records or, whenever we are lucky enough to have a musician among us, "live accompaniment") are often taken from "non-religious" sources which nevertheless seem to echo the symbols and themes of faith. And when we have heard, and sung, we reflect together on these things, in the light of our daily experience. One celebration is especially important for us because, even in the first year, we continued a custom to which several of us had been accustomed in different ways — the yearly celebration of an adapted form of the Jewish Passover celebration, the great feast of freedom. Every year we repeat the ritual prayers, eat the ritual foods that recall the experience of bondage — (the bitter herbs, the saltwater) — and of liberation: the unleavened bread baked from dough that refugees leaving in haste had no time to let rise. Every year we sing the songs of freedom and bless god "for the land and for food!"

The symbol of the bondage in Egypt is vivid, the symbol of Exodus is energizing. That was for us the obvious and earliest symbol. It is from such reading and reflection that the use of these Exodus themes and symbols became inevitable in writing this book. It is natural to us to recognize in the women who are our guests the spiritual sisters of the slaves in Egypt, a whole people rendered landless in order that their labor in the land might enrich and sustain the life-style of those who claimed the land.

We realize that we, and the many others doing similar work, are pushing against a mountain of inertia, of psychic numbness, in a society that, for its own survival, doesn't want to know the kinds of things we are learning and saying, and will go to great lengths to refute them, to explain them away, to blame the victim, or simply not to hear. And on top of this, carefully maintaining the numbness, is the vast superstructure of corporate greed which can only survive by maintaining both oppression, specifically of women, and consumption of the goods it has taught its subjects to want and depend on — and which are affordable because of low wages paid to those who make them, and the ignoring of environmental and health hazards.

To *know* how our society works is to know that the guests in our house are not accidentally poor or abused, but are so because the whole social and economic structure is designed to keep them that way. Not long ago, a group from Wellspring attended a conference on homelessness, at which the keynote speaker was an economist from Columbia University. The main thrust of his address was to point out a popular misconception: we assume that if millions of people are so poor they cannot afford homes that is because somehow the economic system is not working well; there is something wrong with it, therefore it needs to be fixed. The truth is, the speaker told us, that people are poor and homeless because the system is working very well. The system is designed to produce the maximum profit for those who produce goods for sale (whether from manufacture, agriculture, or service industries.) But wages must be kept low to keep prices down and maximize profit, and with the demise of much labor-intensive industry and the rise of "high tech", many workers are no longer needed at all to maintain profits. These people are surplus to the system. The low wages, the unemployment, show the system working as it is designed to work. And, as part of this system, *housing* is a commodity to be bought and sold for profit. Naturally, those who earn little cannot compete in that market. They have no right to housing, they have no title to the land they have been taught to call their own. They may salute the flag but its symbolism of freedom is for them only a comforting delusion.

So the poor are the extras, the leftovers of the system. They have few rights, in practice. Society, feeling uncomfortable at the sight of homeless families, and having failed to conceal their existence entirely, feels obliged to do something — to provide shelter, Welfare payments, subsidized rents which provide access for some to the lowest standard of housing, but which may disappear whenever the landlord decides to sell for condo conversion or to end participation in a subsidy program with all its inspections and restrictions.

The system doesn't change, but makes exceptions, stretches itself a little. "Employment Training" is attached to Welfare payments for women. This is to be "the solution"? But the training is all for low-paid jobs, to keep the system going. The women continue to have the lowest-paid jobs with the least security, and they will therefore be regarded as at least potentially bad parents, in need of "services" to keep them at some minimum level of social acceptability, under threat of losing their children. Also in order to keep those jobs and even to receive the benefits they are "entitled" to they must display at all times attitudes of humility and unquestioning obedience to authority.

What I am describing is, in effect and in detail, a condition of slavery. These are people who are without rights to basic human needs, dependent instead on legal hand-outs and the efforts of non-profit groups (such as Wellspring), people who have no title to land or property, who can be deprived of their children, people who are expected to be "mobile" as the need for cheap labor moves, people who have no security or assured future, people who can be imprisoned either in a mental hospital or a jail if they "over-react" to any of these experiences. Such people are slaves.

It is important for us to recognize, as we wrestle with the nature of Wellspring as a vocation and a way of life, that Moses was not called by God to improve the lot of the people in bondage by negotiating better working conditions or a decent wage. He was sent to call them out of Egypt, because in Egypt they had no ownership in the land. And the lack of ownership was deeply bound up with their ability to worship, to have any sense of God. The Egyptian gods were used to validate the Egyptian power structure, as gods are usually used. The Hebrews in Egypt had a hard time getting in touch with any other kind of God, because they were enslaved spiritually as well as physically. Moses insisted to Pharoah that the people must go out into the wilderness to worship God. Pharoah's early reaction to this was, "Go and offer sacrifice to your God, but in *this* country." And Moses' curious reply was that the ***kinds*** of sacrifice his people would make might outrage the Egyptians, who would stone them. It is an odd but effective way of indicating that the worship offered by free people is simply not possible in a situation of bondage: the oppressors will not allow it because by its very nature it is a statement that the bondage is no longer effective.

The people had to leave Egypt, not just become more comfortable there, because their "salvation" was at stake, the possibility of their becoming people capable of experiencing the spirit which is freedom. Bondage is spiritual, it is deep. The Hebrews had a hard time acclimatizing to freedom, they abused it, they resented it, they pined for dependence, for someone to take care of them. It took a generation to rid them of slavish attitudes, to learn the difference between the autocrat and the leader who is accountable to God and the people. They did not learn this very well and later forgot it, and allowed themselves to be enslaved once more by their own people.

For us at Wellspring it has been important to explore these symbols. They help us to understand the situation we are in and the work we do. The Exodus symbol of bondage and its spiritual results are all too evident around us, and we know, too, how those same symbols have enlightened and energized oppressed people the world over. The means needed for liberation, the difficulties of it, the lingering after-effects of bondage, are all familiar. So is the attraction of the alternative to liberation, by making bondage more comfortable. It is what most slaves want, it is the reason why it is so hard for all of us to envisage freedom as a real option. With the great Passover symbols to focus and energize, the Wellspring experience has meaning, there is a reference point.

But, in the last few years, another kind of symbol has become important, and it is confusingly intertwined with the Exodus symbols. With the years we have become more and more aware of the way in which the root of bondage is simply the lack of ownership in the land in which one lives. And the questions arise not just around the enslavement suffered by the homeless people, (and all the others who are enslaved even if not technically homeless) but around those like ourselves who have a more or less (sometimes less) secure position in society, who are not homeless and have a network of friends to catch them in case of trouble. We are those who are "comfortable", and yet unlike the millions of other "comfortable" people we have a sense of alienation, of not being at home. So the other great biblical theme, that of the Exile, has come to complement (and somewhat confuse) the symbols of Exodus.

For the picture of bondage in Egypt leaves some gaps. It doesn't help us to understand why we feel alienated even when, to some extent, we do have "ownership" in the sense that we know how to work within the system and achieve good things within it. The symbol of the Exile helps to understand this, and I have already been using that kind of language.

The reason the Exile themes help is that the Exile is something that happened to the people of God when they had long possessed their own land. They had fought for it, and settled it with some rather dubious theological justification and considerable cruelty, (really the same justifications and cruelties by which the American land was obtained). But later they had allowed their leaders to become autocrats and to create a self-perpetuating royal and clerical elite. They had allowed their priests to become their masters and to declare a monopoly on access to the God who had led the people to freedom. No longer free, God was contained in the Temple and its elaborate worship and its system of taxation and mandated sacrifice and of atonement for sin (what was, and what was not, sin being decided by the priest, and how much you had to pay, and offer, for cleansing). The parallels with our own situation both in state and church are too obvious to need pointing out.

Because of this, the people lost sight of God, lost the sense of itself as people. No longer one people in intimate relation with God and with the land in which God was encountered, they were open to "foreign gods" and indeed more or less made Yahweh into a "foreign god". They did this, as oppressive regimes have always done, by interpreting the reality of God as a divine validation of the status quo, meaning the power of the powerful and their claim to control the land and its people in God's name. Thus it was that foreign gods, in the form of invaders, were able to take away their land and take them away, too, into exile. The God who had given them a sense of themselves as free people was no longer with them because they had long ceased to believe in that kind of God. So they became exiles, and in exile, at last, some of them began to understand.

In our own countries we are exiles. We have ceased to believe in a God who liberates, which is evident from the way our society is organized. We use the slogans of freedom, as the Israelites did, but we don't create structures that give them reality. We import "foreign gods" and worship them with human sacrifices and build them temples with forced labor from among our own people, and of course we *call* the foreign gods by the name of the God of freedom, so that everyone is confused and protest is muted. Then we lose the land, we are alienated from the sense of who we are as people of the land. We are carried into Exile.

The painful truth of this symbol for our time and people is something we at Wellspring came to realize gradually. It is a hard truth to realize, partly because, of course, we are not literally in a foreign country. Yet, once one gets in touch with the meaning of this the reality is illuminating and shocking. We are *all* exiles, and our vocation is to find the way to come home and to rebuild our homeland. But, as in the case of the people in Babylon, there are many who have so settled into the exile situation, so accustomed themselves to the gods of Babylon and to their values, that they don't feel themselves to be exiles. The old stories of "home" are far off, nostalgic tales of a no doubt heroic world which is past and best preserved in museums and patriotic songs. But still, there are those of us who try to understand how we came to be exiles in our own land, and dream of return, and wonder how to create a new homeland that will not be doomed to repeat all the old mistakes and sins.

So, in this book, I find myself drawing on two sets of symbols, which have obvious affinities but different emphases. Both seem to me to ring true, and both are needed. The great and more familiar stories of the coming out of Egypt, which we celebrate each year at Wellspring at the Seder ritual to which many come, speak to us clearly and energize with hope, but the symbols of Exile are in some ways even more deeply challenging and disturbing to mainly middle-class people who have committed themselves to the task of liberation. Liberation, then, is not just "going *out*", but "coming *home*". And this strange, doubly symbolic enterprise links up with the task of caring for the earth which is our home, and which is in need of liberation from bondage. Without that, we have no place to call home, no place to come back to.

These themes underly the movements of change which are evident all over the world, and of which we at Wellspring are a small part. In order to become part of the movements of change, we ourselves are changed. So it seems important, at this point, to remember some of the ways people in the Wellspring story have changed, and how and why.

CHAPTER TWO

COMING OUT OF EXILE CHOOSING TO CHANGE

Why do people take drastically different directions in their lives, when they aren't obliged to do so? If this book is about exile and the return from exile, why do some people decide they won't tolerate exile while others — like many of the Jews deported to Babylon — have no desire to move, having accepted their immigrant situation and finding it not uncomfortable? This chapter looks at the experience of radical change which created Wellspring, and ponders its roots and its consequences. It looks at particular lives, at their rooting and uprooting, at the choices of home and homelessness, at women and men looking for a place that could embody a vision: exiles deciding to come home.

What are the things that can so disrupt a life that it has to pull up its roots and seek a new place? Illness, or loss of income or some such major force, may change a person's life completely, but although the ways of responding to such drastic enforced change are many, and the choices made at the time are vital to the way that a life develops, the change itself is not optional. What is less explicable is the fact that some people, apparently settled into a reasonably comfortable and useful way of life, choose to take a completely new direction. Some of the people in the Wellspring experience found their lives changed perforce, and most of the guests at the house come into this category, but the group that began and continued the project were not obliged to change, at least in the sense of being victims of external forces. In another sense they were (or so they felt) obliged to change.

Linked to this is the whole question of what is often called "vocation". A person with a strong sense of a need to change direction may identify this as a "calling", perhaps of a specifically religious kind. What is "vocation" or "calling"? How does it happen? The early stages of the

Wellspring experience exhibit some of the dynamics of such a sense of being inwardly obliged to change, or respond to a "calling". For several people, it all began in a small gathering of Christians of a kind which is replicated nation-wide and world-wide.

The Wellspring project emerged from some members of a small group of Christians who met weekly to study Scripture and pray together. The group consisted of ordinary middle-class people, members of an ordinary middle-class parish, owners of small homes, raisers of families, church-goers, capable and intelligent but not obviously adventurous people.

One of them, Mary Jane, was a middle-aged married woman who worked part time in the education office of the parish. She also worked for "Birthright" and was therefore in touch with the struggles of young women faced with unwanted pregnancy. Sometimes she had women in this situation in her home.

Two of the group were religious Sisters, Nancy and Marygrace, who ran the religious education of the parish, and were community leaders in various ways. Marygrace was, at the time the story really began, finishing a doctoral program and only part time in the parish, but very much part of the phenomenon that began to emerge. The other, Nancy, was in fact the major leader in the parish and responsible for the growth of a number of different groups of adult Christians in it — bible study groups, a group of parents of mentally handicapped children, neighborhood groups. The growth of a large and active parish council was also due to her energy and leadership, and the program of religious education for children and young adults with mental handicaps of which the parents group was an offshoot, was also due to her creative energy, at a time when the usual church attitude to such children was to assure the parents they were blessed, and ignore them.

Both women were, in different ways and at different levels of consciousness, dissatisfied with the religious life in which they were still involved, though living independently, as many Sisters did and do. The reason for this alienation, or the development of it, are part of the development of the

Wellspring experience, and part of the wider experience of what "vocation" means. Mary Jane, a married woman who with her husband was also to become one of the Wellspring founders, through working in the education office had become a friend to the two Sisters. She was one of the group which met for study and prayer, and her honesty of vision and integrity of mind and heart were essential elements in the occurrence of the "break" that became Wellspring.

The Scripture study group met in the living room of the little house where Nancy and Marygrace lived, and it was among these people and in this home, within this experience, that something began to stir and to cause changes. The group met weekly, read a passage from the gospels, prepared and presented by members in turn. Members reflected in silence, shared and discussed, prayed and sang songs to music on records, sometimes shared a potluck meal. The group became known as the "Community"; its members became very close to each other.

At one point another component was introduced into the development of the group, one which proved to be crucial. The component was myself, and my own experience of "calling" certainly shaped the impact that I had on people in the group, themselves becoming aware of the initial stage of what was to become radical change. It is therefore necessary to write about what that experience was like for me.

My own life, already rather peculiar from some points of view, had also been subjected to a need for radical change. My family and I had been the initiators of a community experiment in rural Scotland to which we moved in 1974 from the comparative normality of middle class life in a Yorkshire village. The reasons for that change were complex. Some grew from a discontent with that kind of life-style, a middle-class life in a local community semi-attached to and dependent upon a large boys' college run by monks. That educational setup contained all the usual contradictions of "kind good people", "doing a good job" in an institution hopelessly corrupted by its own dependence on wealthy parents and the corporate, academic (to some extent) and military and defense worlds which dictate the terms of education and determine its real, as opposed to its stated, value-system in Western society. Our older children had been influenced by the community movement of the late sixties and its sense of a different possibility. Yet the catalyst, the reason why change became essential was the sadder reason of my husband's problems with alcohol, and the need, as it seemed to us, for a totally different environment if he were to have the possibility of healing. How that happened, the growth and change in that community, the building by our amateur hands of a fifteen-bedroom, two-story log house and farm buildings and the focus on caring for the mentally ill in that supportive environment — all that is another long, extraordinary story. For myself, that major change led to yet further changes, and after seven years, to a choice to leave that community which was to have been the fulfillment of dreams of many years. The reasons for the change are not relevant here, though in retrospect they seem inherent in the personalities and the nature of the experience. That is another story — but it is a story about a *place*, a home, which strove to create a sense of belonging for alienated — exiled — people.

That choice to leave came out of a very clear sense of calling, emerging at a distinct point in my life, after two years of restlessness and a sense of impending change, which I could not pin down. I was unable to make sense of this restlessness, which was in contradiction to all my conscious desires, hopes and plans. During that time a series of dreams, all about giving birth to a baby, indicated the "birth" of a different life, yet it was long before I could accept what was happening. The breakthrough came when the death of my father made it necessary and possible to be away from home to spend time with my younger sister, still living in the old house where my parents had lived since 1950. I found there the distance and space in which to recognize a sense of calling, which I perceived as a call to mission in the context of the emerging Christian communities I had already encountered (during twelve years of lecture tours) in the United States. In retrospect, it seems clear that the religious language of vocation was my "way out". The god-within, stifling and oppressed, was breaking through to a freedom needed for survival. (One of the peculiar marks of that time of breakthrough was that I found myself literally able to breath. Asthma, which had been a permanent feature of my life since childhood, on and off but never totally absent, suddenly ceased.)

At the time that I met the people who were to be the beginnings of the Wellspring experience I was in the middle of changing. I had accepted what I felt was a clear calling to a different way of life, but I was still trying to discern what form that would take — or at least I told myself I was still deciding. In fact I had "decided", and only needed to find adequate religious language and religious imagination to provide a convincing support and context for what was deeply and simply a need for spiritual/personal survival.

Does this perception that a strong sense of religious calling had its roots in a need for psychic survival devalue "vocation"? Or is "vocation" a word for the deep need to reach for a way of life in which a person can find herself, which is also to find the true God? We can create gods to justify our choice of oppression (suffered or imposed) and these are the gods of Egypt. The God of the Exodus is the God we discover when we make the choice for freedom. But living with that God is a very unsettling experience in which all previous religious expectations, acceptances, and concepts are eventually brought in question, including the Exodus experience itself, as indeed the Hebrew people found. This process has been an integral part of the Wellspring experience for those immersed in it.

It happened at the time of this transition in my life that I was invited by the parish, in the persons of Nancy, Marygrace and Mary Jane, to lead a day of reflection for married couples. In preparation for this I met with these three and other parish leaders to plan the day, and in the course of conversation spoke also of my own desire, (articulated out of my new description of what my vocation called me to) after many years of going on the lecture circuit, to spend longer periods with emerging Christian community groups around the country in order to help them identify the meaning and purpose of their experience and move it forward. The kind of parish this seemed to be, with emerging small groups and vital leadership, made me want to continue my contact with it.

So it was that, in the following January, I returned to the parish for a stay of several weeks. Meanwhile, I had made a thirty day-retreat which was intended to be a time for reaching a decision about my future direction. In fact I was already holding fast to the image of that future of which my imagination had been full for months. (The thirty day retreat is one of the religious experiences which I have learned to assess differently by hindsight. At the time it was a marvelous experience, and indeed it brought to the surface many memories and feelings which I was able to accept and integrate into my life in a new way. But it was dangerously self-validating. It reinforced what I wanted to reinforce and gave the power and authority of a religious insight to the fantasies I needed in order to continue in the path I had chosen. It also gave a specious conviction of absoluteness to the lifestyle I wanted and needed at the time. My imagination helped to set me free, but the religious interpretation of it made it hard to judge the real value of my own imaginative constructs. This is, as I have discovered when I shared it with others, a common and even normal experience.

Imagination is the essential tool of liberation. Unless we can imagine something different we remain stuck, which is why revolutions are the result not simply of intolerable conditions, but of intolerable conditions plus a voice that cries out that something else is imaginable and possible, be it the voice of Moses or Marx. But imagination as a tool of liberation is also limited by the scope of the images it uses, and depends for its validity on the closeness of the relationship between the image and the actual contemporary reality — the conditions under which change has to happen. This is why some Marxist-inspired revolutions have either not worked out as liberating, or have been modified, (as in China) to deal with reality in a way the original vision did not encompass.

My own little revolution was in full swing when I came back to the parish, after a difficult Christmas vacation in the community in Scotland, fraught with misunderstandings lightly masked by genuine kindness and good will.

During my time in the parish that winter, while staying in the house where Nancy and Marygrace lived, I met several small groups and led retreats and workshops, learned to recognize the reaching out to new images, the vision of "something else" that stirs in the most unexpected people, though only a few may reach a point where the present situation is clearly named as one of exile, and the nostalgia for "home" translates into decision and action. The bonds of custom, family, religious images and cultural expectations are often too strong.

I joined the Scripture group of which they were part, and led some of the Scripture studies. The whole thrust of my own reading of Scripture, my interpretation of calling, was concerned with the role of small Christian communities and the call to simplicity of life and commitment to the poor. In retrospect I marvel at my own ignorant confidence and simplistic approach. Yet, among a number who heard, in this group and others, and were excited, a few were moved more deeply, because they were at a point in their own lives where they needed to hear a prophetic voice, a voice imagining a different possibility, and not only to hear it but to move to decision in response to it. The limitations of my own state of mind, my own simplification and rationalization, were not immediately important, though some of us had to wrestle with their consequences later.

The personal struggle, this way of dealing with my own need for freedom and growth, was, therefore, deceptive and flawed, but also good and necessary. And there were these other people whose own personal searching for truth had led them to a point where they needed a new direction and were looking for one. Just as I had, they also needed some kind of imaginative construct to give form to their desire.

Someone had to give a name to the restlessness, the vague dissatisfaction. Someone had to say it was OK to feel that way, that in fact it was a spiritually valid experience, that it made sense. Like so many have before us, in seeking to express our sense of direction, we used the hallowed language of the Exodus (the "exile" symbolism had not yet occurred to us) to reflect the experience of calling and change. I don't think any of us were as yet fully in touch with the stark appropriateness of the symbols of slavery, of being aliens, of needing to "leave" the land of oppression. We still thought of the experience of alienation in purely "spiritual" terms. But all those concerned already had, in fact, experienced themselves as becoming gradually aware of "not being at home", as being, in some sense, "homeless", though it was only much later in the Wellspring experience that such thoughts emerged explicitly.

A few years later, when Wellspring House was in existence and welcomed its first group of trainees to the short-lived "Movement for North American Mission", the same phenomenon was very obvious. These trainees were people of different ages and backgrounds, attracted by an advertisement which offered a two year training for mission work in their own country. These were not young people, just out of school, they were men and women already established in careers, and they were an extremely varied group, in an age range from the twenties to the sixties. They were prepared to uproot, to commit themselves to two years of training which involved living and working in very poor areas of the country, doing without financial security for themselves. When they first arrived at Wellspring House for the intensive five-week orientation which began the program, they had never met each other before, and we asked them, in the first days, to tell each other the stories of how they had come to be where they were. It was interesting, as they listened to each other, that the predominant feeling expressed by many was relief. "I'm not crazy after all — there are others who feel the same!"

Each of these men and women discovered what the group which originally began Wellspring had discovered — that their experience of alienation from "normal" life, of inner restlessness, was not unique; that the uneasiness, and the guilt at their own discontent (since they had, after all, a good life) was also part of the pattern; that the reaction of resentment, amusement, contempt, and even abuse from friends, families, employers and clergy was also a recognizable phenomenon in the lives of people afflicted by a sense of calling. To those who feel settled in the land of exile, for whom "home" is merely a nostalgia, the presence of people actually making plans to uproot and seek the "homeland" is very disturbing. It raises up in the minds of the "settled" their own buried discontents and lost dreams, and in order to bury them again they must, in a sense, "bury" those who insist on making radical changes in their own lives and so challenge the validity and worth of those who don't want to change.

What happened in the parish community group was that the study of the radical message of the gospel, served to validate those restless and alienated feelings in some members of the group. The gospel message of liberation and commitment became something people had to deal with more directly. As some grasped the disturbing implications, their visible struggle to deal with the message in their own lives made it more difficult for others to deal with it in a purely "spiritual" way. This sense of discomfort and alienation in what had seemed a reasonably acceptable way of life is the basis of the change traditionally symbolized by the Exodus myth. Slaves, accustomed to that condition and always hoping it will get a bit more comfortable (and sometimes it does) hear a voice that is also their own voice, a voice that makes them aware that enslavement is not the only possible state, that something else is possible, is right, is attainable. It happened to the Hebrews, it happened to the people who gathered around Jesus, it happened to the early Quakers and to many others who began to perceive a different way. Once perceived, the vision allows them no more comfort in the land of enslavement.

The responses to this happening among friends and neighbors were varied, as they are bound to be. Some people found in this time of restless questioning and "opening", the motivation to deepen and clarify existing commitments to practical compassion and work for justice locally. The resettling of a refugee family was a project that sprang from such an experience, and later on the involvement of some in a local meal program for the hungry. Later on some of the group took part in the great Peace Rally in New York in 1982, an experience which in itself helped towards political radicalization; the vision of a different possibility, a different nation, was very clear to those who marched and sang and gathered all day with a million other people — black and white and brown, from other nations and of every conceivable political complexion and point of view. Some also became involved in the Wellspring project in supportive ways, and have continued to be so, becoming increasingly part of the Wellspring experience.

Some found that the challenge of the gospel brought to the surface a sense of being in a dead end, of "stuckness" and alienation which had been part of their lives for some time but not fully recognized. They began to feel that a radically new direction was not only possible but necessary. It was Mary Jane, quiet, self-deprecating, but with the strength of an honest mind, a compassionate heart and a shrewd, accurate and humorous judgement of people, who finally broke things open by actually saying that she couldn't wait any longer, she had to take a new direction, move out, do something different.

For some time before this she and Nancy had shared their conviction that something else was possible and necessary. Marygrace, wanting change, but unsure of her own future direction, shared their searching, needing freedom to discover a different life for herself. Nancy had recognized for over two years that her pioneering and productive work in the parish needed to come to a conclusion. She had attempted to build up a sense of ownership among lay people in the parish; she had empowered many and if they were ever to claim that power they must do it without her. She knew there would be feelings of resentment, hurt and abandonment, but it was clear she should leave. For her personal growth also, she needed to change, to be free to discover something new.

This was in the early spring of 1981. From that time the dynamics of the group changed in ways that can be traced in many similar situations. The would-be pioneers found themselves somewhat isolated. They were supported by friendship and encouragement, at one level, but an unease and nervous apprehension could also be felt, and as the word spread of impending change there were repercussions. There was — there is bound to be — a certain threatening quality in the fact of a person one has known and relied on as "one of us" suddenly showing herself to be, in important respects, different. The difference is acceptable if it is due to sudden wealth, or a better career, or even modest fame by becoming, for instance, an author. It is usually acceptable to religious people if a "vocation" fits the traditional religious models, and means a move into clerical or religious life, or even a spell of volunteer work for the poor. It is much less easy to deal with change if it is toward a lower standard of living, or less security, or something socially peculiar such as community living, but above all it is difficult to deal with if these changes are explained explicitly as an attempt to live the gospel. It is threatening because that seems an implied criticism of everyone else. The underlying, unspoken reaction is "who do they think they are?" Their decision can seem to devalue the life-choices of others, and this is very painful to those who make openly "different" choices. They know so well that others, whose lives may seem unchanged, may have in fact made even more difficult and important choices, but not choices with immediately obvious outward signs. So, added to the doubts and fears in those who choose to make major outward changes is the guilt at feeling that they might seem to be claiming a kind of virtue they know they don't possess, and unintentionally seeming to judge others.

But the negative reaction of those who don't change at all is always there. To give a personal example from long ago, when my husband and I and our family sold our home and started the community in Scotland, slowly building the house there with amateur volunteer labor, the comments in the monastery and the village we had left were not subtle. Common opinion — voiced by monks and neighbors — was that the place was a sex and drug-laden hippie commune: one bright suggestion was that Algy and I had chosen this as a cheap way to have a house built for ourselves!

There are various ways in which people react to the phenomenon of vocation in others. A common one is to dismiss the project as "crazy", and try to bring the afflicted one to a proper sense of responsibility to family, job or church. Jesus himself encountered this reaction, and his family even contemplated confining him until he came to his senses, which he had clearly abandoned. Edwina Gateley successfully founded the Volunteer Missionary Movement in England, when still in her twenties, with the aim of sending lay people to serve as volunteer missionaries in the Third World. It has since indeed sent many thousands and is now established in the United States. But when she was trying to get started she found little support for the idea. The reaction varied from puzzled kindness to impatience and dismissal, and one priest advised her to go home and pray for two years. This is a common response — prayer in this sense being regarded as a kind of spiritual tranquillizer. The method is to deal with the change of another's radical commitment by asserting that nothing can be done without much prayer; one must wait on the Spirit, wait for God to "give a sign". It is true that this can be a wise awareness of the need for real openness, (such as I personally certainly lacked!) but equally it can be a way of blocking change, because "signs" come to those who really want them. The proliferation of retreat centers in the last decade, an amazing array of books and cassettes on prayer and the development of a great range of new "spiritualities" and different prayer and meditation techniques with interesting names, may be a healthy sign of a more reflective and less routine religious practice. A more cynical view might suggest that it is also a reaction to a world in which the media-demonstrated existence of gross poverty and oppression alongside, and supporting, an affluent life style, makes it increasingly difficult for religious people in comfortable circumstances to avoid the practical implications of the gospel call to discipleship. A lot of praying is one way to do that, if prayer becomes an occupation, rather than a life.

Yet the discomfort of those dealing with someone else's "vocation" is often fruitful. In the case of the Wellspring pioneers, it provided an important opening up for others; it relieved the sense of being locked into a religious system. It offered a kind of window onto a wider horizon. What all of these people were dealing with — those who reacted positively and those who didn't — was the old problem about people with "vocations" when vocation takes the form of a sudden and radical change in life-style. Those who cannot take that way for all kinds of adequate reasons are challenged to re-examine the assumptions — religious and cultural — on which their chosen life style if based. Some respond to the challenge, find it stimulating and liberating, discover ways to make the way of life in which they must continue responsive to the insights they receive. This happened to many who were supporters of the Wellspring pioneers, and later became a significant part of the wider network of Wellspring as it developed. Others are so threatened that they can only reject the challenge, either by denying the validity of the vocation they perceive (clergy often do this) or by fudging the issue by means of religious activities of a less disturbing kind.

From the time of Jesus (and indeed the prophets before him) through the stories of every individual or group which has moved away from the accepted church structure and patterns of the time and chosen a different life-style in the name of the gospel, the reactions have been similar. On the one hand there has been enthusiasm, a sense of liberation and tremendous hope and energy, leading to profound personal change, whether uprooting and "following" on the path of mission, or by change within the given situation. This latter was the way taken by so many households of early followers of Jesus, households which became transformed from within into what were later to become "house-churches", centers of hospitality, faith and service of the new "Way". At the time of the great Franciscan movement, not only those who left everything and followed Francis were affected, but thousands of people whose ordinary domestic and working lives were transformed and transfigured by this experience, which put them in touch with a very different kind of God from the God of judgement and law they had previously known. On the other hand there has always been the other reaction of suspicion, anger, rejection, ridicule and persecution even to death. People who change when others don't are not easy to live with.

Yet they almost can't help themselves. Once the insidious message has found a way in, its resonance cannot easily be muffled. Persuasion is tried, or offers of more money if one stays in the existing job. Heart-rending pictures are painted of the future of bereft families, or fellow workers, of projects falling apart, of work left in the hands of the incompetent, or of scandal caused to the "weaker brethren", who are always brought in to support the argument for inaction. Yet there is a kind of momentum of the imagination which cannot be stopped. One can imagine the period of decision for the Jews in Babylon, whose faith had been nurtured with prophetic images of forgiveness and the promises of return to their own land. The dream became a possibility when Cyrus gave permission, encouragement and money for resettlement (and he must have experienced some judicious pressure from wealthier and influential Jews, as well as, perhaps from their business rivals). Then they had to decide whether to make the vision a reality; they were settled, often prosperous — after all it had been the "cream" of the nation, its intellectual elite and leaders that had been deported. It was not easy to leave everything they had created in two generations, to return to the "home" they had never seen. But the dream called them, and many responded.

With the people who were to be Wellspring, in the middle of all this sense of hope, excitement, fear, dreaming, praying, someone else came into the scene. She literally came through the door, one snowy night a year after my own first visit to the parish. The doorbell rang in Nancy and Marygrace's house, the house which was then the center of the whole story. On the doorstep stood a tear-stained girl of seventeen in a light jacket. Nancy knew her from her involvement in parish programs. Nancy cried, "Jane, what's the matter?" and she replied "Everything!" and almost fell into Nancy's arms, sobbing and shaking. When she stopped shaking enough to speak, bits of the story came out, a long story the whole of which only emerged later, a story which had brought her to a point where she knew that if she went back this time, she would never have the strength to run away again. Much of her story cannot be told here. It is enough to say that it is the kind of story which we have heard many times at Wellspring. Nancy put Jane into a hot bath and then into one of her own nighties and her own bed. Jane did not go home again.

Jane's coming suddenly gave a very concrete form to the new sense of direction which was being tentatively and privately discerned. There are many "Janes" who on winter nights, or any other nights, have nowhere to go but back into an intolerable situation. Something might be done for a few of them.

Chance? A sign from God? An event, at any rate, which had special significance because of what was already being shared and dreamed. A few weeks earlier my own share in the shaping of the dream had taken on a new force. It had been during the fall of 1980 that on an unexpected day off, Nancy and I had time to dream about what form our future work together might take. By that time I had been back to the parish, between visits to other groups and communities in the United States and in Canada, and Nancy and I had become good friends. We wanted to work together in some way, but I was not at all clear how, because I had imagined myself continuing to travel most of the time, spending weeks with different communities in different areas, rather in the model of St. Paul! But Paul, besides being tougher and a lot younger than I was, normally settled in and made a home for months on end, a point my fantasies had not considered. Nancy's idea, while not excluding travel, was that a base was needed, a place to work and live together with others, a place for people in need to come. As she talked about it, my own images shifted and changed. I caught her dream and dreamed it too.

It became less a dream and more a necessity when the effect on myself of non-stop travelling became apparent. Before Christmas, when I was due to return to England to my family, I went on a shopping expedition — and did nothing but cry uncontrollably. Stress, and anxiety brought on by refusing to recognize my own physical and emotional limitations, had exposed the limits of the image which had enabled me to break free. Its validity had been in its power to energize and liberate. It was not sufficiently in touch with reality to allow it to provide a whole way of life, which is what I had tried to make it do. Fortunately, at the moment when reality, in the form of physical and emotional exhaustion, broke in, I was offered an alternative, a way to live out the calling in its essentials, but in a context which could provide the support and sharing that I needed, but thought I could do without. Thus, another part of the picture became clear.

A place of hospitality, a community life, a refuge for the homeless, a base, also, for some kind of mission — the picture was becoming clearer. It was then, early in 1981, that we began to speak of it not as a possibility, but as a clear intention. Another person, Jenny, came into it too, a Sister of the Congregation to which Nancy and Marygrace belonged, wanting to return to Massachusetts to be near her mother, but also wanting a change from teaching, a different lifestyle. Mary Jane's husband, Paul, was also taking early retirement from one job and unclear about his direction. We were all talking, discussing possibilities. It was Mary Jane who finally said, "We can go on talking forever. We must find a house."

The moment when the momentum of imagination carries the scene to the point of action is crucial. Mary Jane was right. One can go on talking, dreaming, praying — and procrastinating, but concrete action pins down a project in unexpected and disconcerting ways. The fact is that the activity is never exactly what was envisioned, and may lead in entirely new directions. Fidelity to the vision may actually mean changing the form of it; in my own case I had had to change it in order to survive.

The moment of action for the Wellspring group was the decision to buy the house: *the* house, not *a* house. One can go on looking for the ideal house for a long time but when one particular house is chosen, all the other possible houses — and therefore the form of project they might have made possible — evaporate. There is something very sobering about signing a purchase and sale agreement!

The peculiarity of this particular purchase was that none of the seven people directly involved in the project had any available capital and all of them were either jobless or about to be jobless. But the peculiarity began before that. The house itself was "discovered" rather than sought, when Nancy and I took a ride to the ocean one sunny April day, just to get away from the telephone. Taking a back route into Gloucester, we saw it — old, solid, comfortable, and with a "For Sale" sign up. Nancy made a U-turn in the road and demanded that I make a note of the Realtor's number. Then, without speaking, we headed for down-town Gloucester and stopped on Main St. At this point Nancy's courage forsook her. What kind of reception would we get — two women with no money, no credentials, wanting to see a large and no doubt expensive house? We didn't find the realtor advertised on the house. Instead, we walked along, peered into the windows of one realtor's office, didn't like the look of it, walked on and plunged hastily up the stairs to another, because it had a woman's name on it. That seemed a little less daunting.

We summoned up all available dignity and self-confidence and explained that we were interested in a large house which could provide a place for people in need of some quiet and support. It was all rather vague. This was in 1981 and at that time nobody was talking about homelessness, except the people who ran the few shelters, mainly for single men, such as Pine Street Inn in Boston. Homelessness did not then appear in the headlines, and most people either didn't know about it or didn't want to. So we were not entirely disingenuous; at that stage we envisaged offering short live-in retreats, or space for people needing a quiet respite from difficult home lives. But hospitality to people in need was the central idea, and we knew many of them would be poor.

We looked through folders of details and pictures of a number of houses, most of them at prices which made us blink, though we tried to look nonchalant, as if buying houses for two or three hundred thousand were an everyday affair. Then we found the page — and there was "the" house, the one we had seen. This Realtor also had it on her books.

The price of it was high, but not as high as some, and we didn't have any money anyway, so a few thousand more or less didn't signify. We arranged to view several houses, including "the" one, not wanting to trust our first enthusiasm too much. Then we sped home to tell the others. A few days later three of us looked at four different houses. Two had poky rooms, though lots of them, and one was zoned for one-family dwellings. The fourth was the one we had sighted by chance. We walked in through the side door and a swallow flew out of its nest in the car port. We felt it was a good omen, for we knew it was the right place. Nancy did a little war dance on the brick floor of the sun-porch. "I want it, I want it!", she said, expressing the feelings of the other two.

On Monday after Easter five of us looked at it. We raised difficulties on purpose in order to be able to overcome them. We tramped through the house, peered up into the huge brick fireplace, climbed the steep rocks behind the house. Built originally in 1649 it had sheltered many generations, seen many births, matings and deaths. It had been built, we learned, by some of the earliest English settlers, later home to a black family of freed slaves. There were photos of their descendants on the walls. Once it was an inn. Extended and restored since then, it seemed to wait for new life.

That day the whole group, somewhat dazed and feeling a need for time to think, went and drank some remarkably bad coffee in a diner. It was Paul who said, "What are we going to offer for it?" A question which somehow jumped over the other question of whether we should make an offer at all. We made an offer, conditional on the sale of Paul and Mary Jane's house, the proceeds of which they planned to use for part of the purchase. Next day I left for England, but a few days later I received a call to say that Mary Jane and Paul had put their house on the market immediately, although everyone said it was a bad time to sell and they would have to wait weeks, and get a low price. They sold it two days afterwards to the second viewer at the asking price. Meanwhile, Nancy and Marygrace's Congregation proved willing to hold a mortgage at low interest. So the money was available. It was all a little frightening; the dream was grounded in a solid old house, and the house seemed right, but were we?

As a symbol of what the group was about, and what it was to discover, the old building was powerful. The original builders had been, like ourselves, people with a vision yet very practical.

The house holds stories of risk and discovery, of love and fear and hope. On that day in April in 1981, it was chosen to become a place of many more stories and discoveries. It was to become the new land, the place to learn freedom and unlearn much else, and to discover the meaning of "land".

Would the rather vague sense of calling measure up to the reality of living together and supporting the house financially? In meetings beforehand we had formed ourselves into a corporation (non-profit status was still down the road) and agreed each to contribute $500 a month out of our earnings, to support the house. So as long as each of us had a part-time job of some kind we could pay our way. The early weeks were exciting — and funny, and memorable.

One precious experience was the general enthusiasm and support of many people in the parish that Nancy, Marygrace and Mary Jane were leaving. A small army of women armed with buckets, scrubbing brushes and various cleaning agents descended on the house and over several days scrubbed it from top to bottom. (Having been inhabited previously by four bachelors and four Persian cats, this was very necessary.) The sense of community which had grown through shared Scripture study and shared work in the parish endured the move. Among many, the initial doubts and pulling back were less strong than friendship and real care for those venturing into this new life.

There is something in this surge of supportive enthusiasm which has to do with the experience of radical change. For those who are touched by it, it is not only challenging, it can be energizing, bringing a feeling of new life. The experience of watching the beginning of a visible, concrete project like the Wellspring one goes beyond the challenge I spoke of earlier, in response to another's sense of vocation. This is a further stage; it is the fact — seen, touched,shared — that something different is possible. It relativizes the sense that one's life is fixed, that home, church, career, are unchangeable walls closing off options. One may choose to remain within them, but that is choice, not fate, and the fact of choice transforms the experience of life within them. It gives a feeling of ownership, of being rooted in a deeper reality, and this had much to do with the questions we were to raise later, those which eventually led to this book. What is it that gives "ownership"? Is it simply paying for, *owning* a piece of land in the legal sense? Is it feeling responsible for it? Is it feeling oneself part of the history of a place, a group, a nation? Surely it has, at least, some quality of *choice,* of not being constrained but able to decide, to be there because one feels it matters.

This was the experience of the Wellspring pioneers. It was a frightening yet exhilarating experience to move in, to begin to live the daily routine in this new place and secretly wonder if it could possibly work, if the ordinariness of getting up and showering, cleaning, shopping, beginning to arrange the rooms, was really as ordinary and safe as it seemed.

In some ways it hadn't been ordinary anyway. Because the buyer of Mary Jane and Paul's house wanted to move in quickly, they had to move out, but there were long delays before closing on the new house. Title searches went on lengthily as lawyers expensively unearthed amazing dynastic disputes going back into the seventeenth century. (One owner had several children, then his wife died, he remarried and had some more. There was a dispute over which wife's children should inherit!) So, with the previous owner's permission, the furniture was moved into three rooms in the house.

The move was done by friends with a huge U-Haul. It was loaded up one evening, and afterwards the little army of movers ate enormous pizzas in the emptied living-room of Mary Jane and Paul's house, where (since all the furniture had gone), a ladder on the floor was used as a table. Next day the gang of helpers stacked all the furniture in the designated rooms in the new house and returned for a celebrating cook-out in the yard of Nancy and Marygrace's little house. Meanwhile, Mary Jane and Paul and their dog crammed into a cousin's house, where no dogs were allowed, and Max, the dachshund, had to be smuggled in and out. But eventually the real moving in happened, after titles to no less than seven parcels of land had been searched and established, and the lawyers had written a book several inches thick. (At one point we owned the land on which half of the house was built, but not the other half, because of the time when the hosue was occupied on two different families, with complicated histories.)

During the weeks of waiting, while the house contained Mary Jane's and Paul's furniture but no bodies, a statue of Mary belonging to Mary Jane's family stood outside at one corner of the house, large and white and obvious. One of the vendors was a Mason; he called our lawyer to enquire what this woman was doing on what was still his property! Possibly, this presence of a symbolic woman in the front yard was an omen — anyway, she stayed there. Eventually the real move-in happened, with first Mary Jane and Paul more or less camping out in the empty house, until gradually the others gathered.

This is a book about the homelessness of women, and the stories in it are therefore mainly about women, and the original group consisted of six women and one man — Mary Jane's husband, Paul, who had the courage to choose to share the venture, at the risk of being regarded by other men as eccentric and foolish. And this presence of a man was important. It is extremely difficult for a representative of the "owners" to join forces with the "owned", and the resistance to it is both interior, from the conditioning that boys and men receive, and exterior, from a society that is liable to regard them at least tacitly as traitors whose behavior threatens the control of the dominant class. Once, white people who showed friendship to blacks were called "nigger lovers" and mocked, shunned, even violently attacked. The same feeling, that such behavior threatens ownership, is present (though more politely) in attitudes to men who take a feminist viewpoint or even work with a high proportion of women. Paul was teased, and it was friendly but sometimes there was an edge to the humor, a kind of mock sympathy that was uneasy. At first, too, some automatically assumed that Paul was in charge of the household — one building contractor, faced with women who knew what they wanted and what they were talking about, and who dared to question his work or his figures, angrily demanded to speak to "the boss!" It was not easy to convince him that Paul was not "the boss" and not easy for Paul (a man accustomed to being in authority) to accept this kind of situation.

Yet ultimately, if the owned are to become co-owners, then the owners must also come to envisage and want co-ownership. It has been important to Wellspring women to share the mission with men, but not many have the mixture of courage, sensitivity and insight needed. In another chapter is told the story of a man who was part of the mission training program and who chose to work with prostitutes, the most "owned" of all women. In the early years of Wellspring's story it was very important that one man shared his life with Wellspring for two years.

Mark is an Episcopal priest who had chosen ordination after a career as a professional singer. At the time he made contact with Wellspring he was working in a parish in Lawrence. Nancy and I were doing some workshops and talks in Boston and elsewhere (as we have continued to do) and in that first year we began to notice one particular bearded face appearing frequently in our audiences. Eventually Mark introduced himself and asked if he could visit. He came, and made himself loved immediately because of his warmth and enthusiasm. He wanted, he said, to join the community.

It was arranged that he should visit a few times so that we could get to know each other; and within a few months he moved in. The church he was serving said goodbye to him with a service of blessing and sending, and for a while he continued to work at a soup kitchen in Lawrence called "Bread and Roses".

Mark's experience had the marks of an exile choosing to come home: the restlessness and unease, the searching and dreaming, the discovery of something that seems to focus the dreams and give direction. But, as a man, he had particular difficulties and a particular kind of value. For guests the experience of living in the house with a man who was gentle and compassionate and yet very masculine was so strange as to be, at first, sometimes unacceptable. It didn't seem to them normal for a man to live among women as an equal, without dominating. But it was a very important experience which opened up new possibilities and was part of their own changing.

Mark was with us in a period of rapid development and learning. He was here at the time when most of us had outside part-time jobs and used the money to support the house; Mark worked in a candy-factory — not most people's idea of what a priest should be doing. Together we worked through the early challenges and changes discussed in this book. Eventually Mark became engaged and married another Episcopal priest, Margaret Rose. Their continued friendship has meant that, although Mark no longer lives here, the contribution of both to the development of the house has been major. For Mark married a feminist — and the two of them have been a part of the ongoing conversation about the nature of feminism and what that means at Wellspring. Sometimes they share worship at Wellspring, at Christmas or Easter, or other times. Often they celebrate feasts with us and Mark's music (so much missed since he left) fills the house as everyone sings. Sometimes there are quieter days for talk and reflection. Their second child was baptized at Wellspring, they share Passover with us. Their journey as a family, experiencing exile and beginning the long trek towards home, has been part of the Wellspring journey also. Mark has been a member of the Board of Directors, and as he himself was working in sheltering in various capacities he has brought insights from that experience. Margaret Rose, dealing with the challenge and joy and pain of being a woman in official church ministry, and the issues raised by being a feminist mother, has contributed to the profound changes in understanding that have taken place. Together, we have perceived land-marks on the journey and known we were going in the right direction.

Perhaps the clearest learning that emerges from the experience of working with Mark, and later with Mark and Margaret, is that changing is something we do together, changing each other and helping each other to discover the next part of the road home, which is often hard to find, obscured by disuse, the fog of misleading values and ideas, or even what seem to be impassable barriers. Together, in the wide variety of people for whom Wellspring is a place for the home-coming venture, we can deal with the challenges and allow ourselves to change.

A major change which came about in the early years at Wellspring was the decision of both Marygrace and Nancy to leave the religious congregation to which they had belonged for all of their adult lives. There were different reasons, and the experience of Wellspring was only part of the decision in each case, yet it was important that Wellspring provided an experience of community, which, with its mixture of companionship, struggle, celebration, failure, achievement, anxiety and hope, was basically real and had meaning. In contrast the experience of religious life as it had become for them did not carry much conviction. In a way, the early Wellspring experience recalled the early years of that, and so many other, religious orders and congregations, and it made it clear that no tradition can count on continued liveliness and power; it has to be constantly questioned, challenged and renewed. The change for both women was painful, because of the hurt to others, the sense of waste from choices made that seemed good at the time, the awareness of past accepted oppression, and the fading of a vision once clear. The change took time, and was hard, but liberating in the end. It mattered to be, at this time, a lay person, one with other ordinary people trying to do something not very ordinary. A year or so later Marygrace married, and her husband, Don, a Lutheran minister and a therapist, has been another strong and important element in the thinking and understanding, the ongoing changes. Their happiness together, their friendship and support (which began with a wonderful wedding party at Wellspring) are part of the journey home.

So, in those first four or five years, the household grew in clarity of purpose and went through some painful experiences. Twice, people came to share the work who seemed just right, but in the event had their own agenda which threatened to absorb all the energies of the community. This was frightening but also clarified the sense of what was really required of us if we were to do the work. The household also rejoiced in the growing circle of friends and supporters, in the happiness of guests finding new homes and new lives, and in the acquiring of the two other houses which now provide permanent homes for low-income men and women.

Because of all this, and much more that cannot be told here, either for lack of space or because it would not be appropriate, the changes in the community have been profound. New people came, and stayed — Mary Kay, back from working in Appalachia, joined the community as Family Life Advocate, working with the families on many issues, drawing on her experience and skill. Maura from Ireland came later, two years after a summer of volunteering here. Donna, herself once a single parent on Welfare, came to work for us in housing search and training the women in finding and keeping homes, dealing with landlords and the law — a very empowering job. Nicole, so far our only long-term Gloucester resident, came to bring many gifts and new enthusiasm. Each person changes everyone else, and becomes part of the discovery and the conversation and the further change. So there we were, not admitting to each other how it felt, and the doubts that niggled.

The changes we made and experienced changed us. Change works inward, and then outward. We see visions, and try to actualize them, and the act changes the seer, and so again the vision is changed. It becomes very important to keep in touch with that original vision, to recognize what in it is central and unchanging, yet how it needs to be modified. This is why, after eight years, the Wellspring group (with only three of its original members, and all those new faces) pulled out its first vision statement, and a later one as well, and raised funds to hire a firm of consultants. To implement the original vision now meant, we knew, to rediscover it in terms of past experience and present needs. So we began, together with the Board of Directors and volunteers, to create a plan for the years ahead, and the plan looks different from anything we envisaged in those first days. And one of the reasons it looks different is the way we have grown theologically and spiritually in response to the experience. At the heart of that is the issue of people without land, the poor who are aliens in their "own" country.

We knew that to insist on carrying through the original vision according to the way it was first imagined can petrify the experience, so that the actualizing of it becomes not so much the realization of the vision, as a deadening kind of play-acting. This is what has happened to many religious orders who insist on continuing to live the vision in terms of the way it was first embodied, in a way of life which no longer makes contact with reality. The true vision is lost. A good example is the radical monastic experiment of the Ephrata community in Pennsylvania, which seems to have come to an end for this kind of reason. The founder, one of the leaders of the great wave of Protestant sectarians which swept over eastern America in the eighteenth century, (the Moravians, Amish, Mennonites and others) wanted to create an ideal community of celibate men and women, and families as well. The life was an extremely austere reworking of Catholic monastic traditions with the Protestant mystical one. The life was planned down to the last detail to embody the founder's vision, but for this very reason it did not long outlast his powerful personality. It made no provision for the ongoing translation of the original vision in terms of changing culture, needs and insights, so it could not adapt, and the vision was lost.

So the original vision may seem, in practice, not to fit the actualities, or may run into problems that make aspects of it seem unworkable. But the temptation then is to assume that the vision is mere fantasy, and must be set aside in favor of a more easily workable project. This is the kind of tragic fate which has overtaken many religious movements, including Christianity, and movements and sects within Christianity. The early church itself, as it spread into the gentile world and was faced with the problem of being acceptable in a hostile environment, quickly let go the radical aspects of the social restructuring which had gone on around Jesus, and in the very early days of the mission.

The church adapted itself successfully to the patriarchal culture of the time, and those groups which tried to hold onto an earlier vision were marginalized as heretical. These groups themselves did not, in fact seek to recover the prophetic social agenda of Jesus. This was in practice unlikely, since they were generally not in touch with Jewish prophetic spirituality and had no first-hand knowledge of Jesus. They tried rather to recapture the euphoric, spirit-filled time of equality, generosity and spontaneous mission of the first days of the church. And these groups themselves, in their efforts to cling to the radical gospel, often made the other mistake, trying to freeze the experience of prophetic leadership, of fraternal and sororal solidarity, of simplicity and reliance on the spirit. Unable to adapt, they eventually died out, or were helped on their way out by vigorous persecution by the (by then) "orthodox" church.

That is the challenge of change. "Without a vision, the people die", but we are not good at understanding the relation between the vision and the reality. We do not recognize the conditions under which the one can become the other, and fail to realize how the vision can remain valid as the reality changes, or else we assume that if we *claim* the authority of the vision, then what we do is bound to reflect it. Even this brief recollection of what happened to the early church is enough to show how fatal that assumption can be.

Simplistic attempts to use Scripture as a manual of behavior will not work either. Apart from anything else, people who do this pick and choose the parts of Scripture they want to obey, and the choices they make betray the underlying unconscious cultural or religious criteria they apply to Scripture. The value system developed in this way is not scriptural, it is cultural, but as that is never admitted there is no self-criticism and no ability to make realistic connections between Scripture and the contemporary experience. Experience is wrenched, rationalized and compressed to fit a notion of Scripture which has no basis in Scripture itself.

What is needed by people who take the gospel demand seriously is a thoughtful and ongoing attempt to understand the vision of a transformed earth and heaven that Jesus was proclaiming, but to understand it as he himself was obliged to actualize it in terms of his own cultural and religious experience. This means we need to be in touch with the basic elements which, to him, were the necessary experiences of the fact of God's reign, the jubilee vision, the breaking in of divine energy to heal and transform land, people, community and culture. We are in touch with this only, of course, through the medium of the writers, themselves writing thirty or more years later for congregations whose experiences, cultures and spiritual needs were very different from those of the original hearers (and rememberers) of the message of Jesus. So the task of re-envisioning the vision of Jesus is not easy — yet when we allow ourselves to read and hear with informed imagination the message does come through with tremendous force and clarity. It seems paradoxical yet appropriate that now, when the world seems farther than ever before from a capacity to express the vision of Jesus, and at a time of unique peril for the earth and its creatures, we have historical, anthropological, literary and linguistic tools to enable us to get in touch with the original vision of Jesus in a way never possible since he proclaimed it. His message can (if we wish to hear) become clearer to us than to any generation since the first.

Basic to the vision of Jesus was the idea that the poor should recover the land which had been taken from them. By this recovery of land Jesus does not appear to have meant getting rid of the Roman occupation, indeed there is little evidence that he thought this significant. To judge by his encounter with the Centurion, for instance, he seems to have been prepared to respect and even like an individual Roman, and to appreciate him simply as a human being, and his attitude to Pilate seems to indicate sorrow at his blindness and a refusal to engage in a dead-end discussion, rather than an outright rejection of the Roman, as such. Jesus was much more concerned with the failure of his own people to be faithful to the vision of the prophets. His call to the rich young man was not to surrender property for the sake of personal poverty as if that were a virtue but to "give it to the poor". The "weak" or "those of gentle spirit", he said, should "inherit the earth", and the poor to whom the "kingdom of Heaven" belongs are those who will inhabit that transformed society which Isaiah envisioned, in which God "reigns" and there is peace and prosperity and long life, when God's kingdom comes "on earth".

Jesus called his people and (as he came in touch with them) all people, to a sense of the earth as the place capable of being God's dwelling, therefore a place of justice and prosperity shared among all. The rain which falls "on the just and the unjust" is the rain that causes the crops to grow, so that people may be fed — all people, not just those who have claimed possession for an elite and made the rest into dependents, aliens in their own land. Anxiety about food and clothing is inappropriate, and hoarding of goods is futile, not because earthly life is unimportant but because in the reign of God, God's people naturally share — so "set your mind on God's kingdom and justice before all else, and all the rest will come to you as well."

At this distance, since all our evidence was put together by people with a different agenda, it is hard to discern what relationship Jesus perceived between earthly life and life after death, of which he never spoke explicitly but only by implication. What is clear is that concern for one was not exclusive of the other — quite the contrary. It seems that he possibly envisioned a breaking in of divine power which would do away with death altogether, though this may be more the vision of his followers than his own. But the central thrust of his public mission seems to have been the proclamation of the jubilee year ("the year of God's favor") in which debts are cancelled, land restored to those who have lost it, exiles return and all declare dependence on, and confidence in, the bounty of God in the fertile earth, beyond even the results of human labor. The jubilee was enjoined by the Torah to occur every fifty years, and to be a "sabbath of sabbaths" in which people, animals, and land should rest and rejoice. Central to it was the proclamation of liberty (Leviticus 25:8 etc.). "You shall proclaim liberty throughout the land . . . and everyone shall return to his own possessions," and "you shall not oppress one another", but deal with fairness, and ways to do this are set out in detail, "for I am your God". The land is God's land and therefore liberty and justice dwell in it and all its inhabitants shall "dwell in it in safety." Those who, through poverty, have lost land once theirs shall regain it. Even the stranger is to be ensured a home, the slave is to be freed and returned to ownership of land with all his family.

This is the mission of Jesus, and his proclamation of forgiveness, peace, reconciliation and nonviolence are all aspects of this. We are talking, therefore, of a gospel in which the subject of the use and abuse of land is cental. This is not a peripheral "political" matter, not even a matter of doing justice as an obligation laid on the religious person. It is the heart of the gospel. Yet when the gospel came to be proclaimed after the departure of Jesus the message was very soon presented as primarily one of spiritual liberation, and the establishment of God's reign as something that would be done from outside by God at some cataclysmic moment not far off. While waiting for that, matters of internal justice and care within the believing community were very important, but there seems to have been no sense at all that the proclamation of the gospel had anything to do with establishing a new social order. This was probably inevitable because the people to whom the message was proclaimed in the gentile world, whether they were Jews of the diaspora, or "Greeks", experienced themselves as powerless before the entrenched systems of injustice and oppression which appeared eternal and inscrutable. Jesus could envisage change in a way his followers could not. What they did grasp was the possibility of a personal liberation which would enable them to experience themselves as free people, no matter what their social condition. This, indeed, had been at the center of Jesus' message, but for him the change of heart was part of the total and cosmic change, whereas later it appeared to be only a way to prepare for it, whether at the "coming of the Lord" or at one's own death.

Soon, as the church grew ever more settled within the cultural community, older patterns of ordering superseded the team ministry and decision-making of the earliest days, and the growing church took on the structures which were nearest to hand, a mixture of synagogue government and the patriarchal culture shared by Jews and Gentiles alike. But the original vision was one of the real *possibility* — not certainty — of radical social change centered on the establishment of justice and compassion in the land, experienced as home for all people.

The gospel message, as the Wellspring group came to perceive it, was about a possibility which can be grasped and made actual, the possibility of a different world, a world in which God is free among the people, in which the energy of life (which is God) flowing between human beings, and through them and in all creation, is not blocked, distorted or ignored.

It was this fundamental sense that something different is possible which underlay the Wellspring venture. The whole project grew from a deep awareness of both the unalterable inter-relatedness of human life with all life and being, and of the fact that our society is based on values which are blind to that inter-relatedness, which magnify competition and the domination of one by another, and an "independence" which denies that need for each other which is inherent in being human and earthly. The touchstone of the vision which fired our imagination was the gospel proclamation of a transformed human and earthly community in touch with the life of God as its own life, and open to the responsibility and opportunity that goes with that awareness.

The working out of that awareness in terms of responding to the needs of the people who, very soon, began to come to the house has been, and still is hard work. It involves a constant re-examination of events, methods, projects and hopes in the light both of experience and of the vision itself. We must judge and learn from mistakes, we must not be afraid to make drastic changes if we feel we have been moving in a wrong direction through failure of insight or courage. One of the biggest changes in the way the work was done began to develop when experience shattered illusions and revealed very clearly what kind of work we had taken on. The story has two layers: "what happened" in the sense of what the newsletters we began to send out to our friends were saying, and what happened to us spiritually and ideologically — in ways we have only been able to recognize by hindsight.

CHAPTER THREE
HOSPITALITY AND RAGE

Seven people moved into the house in the summer of 1981, and began to put the furniture in place, weed the existing flower beds, and even plant a garden. They also began to try to work out the meaning of what the original vision statement claimed as Wellspring's basic principle: hospitality. The seven were Nancy and Marygrace, Paul and Mary Jane, Jeanette (known to us as Jenny, a Sister in the same Congregation as Nancy and Marygrace), myself and Jane. Jane was eighteen by then, and when she heard what we were planning she asked to come too, having no other home once the little house in Peabody ceased to be home for Nancy and Marygrace. "We want you to come," Nancy told her, "as one of the community." So Jane came, and brought to the adventure her youth, and her own experience of rejection, and of new beginning through the hospitality of Nancy and Marygrace. We did not know, then, how appropriate her experience was to seem: one of the dispossessed, the land-less and unwanted, she, and we, had to learn how hard it is for those who have been oppressed to envisage anything else, and yet how, through trials and failures, it is possible to hold onto a new vision.

We decided soon after moving in to put in extra bedrooms in an empty loft area over the carport, since the main house was not big enough to accept more than a very few guests. (Paul borrowed money on his own investments, which we repaid over the next five years.) This naive decision brought us up against the reality of our new city. An irate building inspector, seeing signs of carpentry, came by to ask where was our building permit? When we filled in the necessary forms we got the permit, but were informed that we still needed an occupancy permit to allow any but ourselves to live in the house, since we were already over the limit of "unrelated adults" who were permitted to occupy one house. "You can build anything you like, but there's no way I'll give you an occupancy permit," were the cheery words of the Building Inspector, who added plaintively, "Why did you have to choose Gloucester?" The dynamics behind this discouraging reaction, we discovered, had to do with the presence in Gloucester of the Unification Church (the "Moonies") whose activities had made them unpopular, an unpopularity exaggerated by the tendency of local politicians to make them the scape-goats for any ills the city might suffer. The notion was that we, too, were some kind of sect. What else could we be, all these "incomers" living together and proposing to take in people in crisis? Please go somewhere else. "But", added the Inspector conscientiously, "you can take my decision to appeal."

This we did, but before that we did something else that helped to establish a style that was basic to our understanding of our mission. We invited the neighbors to visit; and talk over our hopes and plans. Not all came, but those who did were, and remained, supportive, and they spoke to others. We also introduced ourselves to local human service agencies. At this stage they didn't take us very seriously, but they were friendly. So, when our application for an occupancy permit (as a lodging house, the only category that seemed to fit) came before the City, the council chamber was full of supporters, and the only opponent publicly withdrew his opposition, saying that he felt like a lion who was unable to roar! When the Council handed down a decision in Wellspring's favor the cheering and clapping was so prolonged that the Chairperson had to request that the celebration be continued elsewhere, so that business could continue.

So we were legally established, and one reason for the favorable verdict was another decision which also grew from conviction: we committed ourselves to paying 100% property tax although our non-profit status (which we had gained by then) could have exempted us from that obligation. That commitment expressed our sense of belonging to the local community and therefore wanting to contribute to it. That decision was another of those conclusions arrived at intuitively which only later appeared to be an integral part of an emerging theology.

(The story of how we got our non-profit status, with the help of Marygrace's lawyer brother, is another one too long to tell here. Enough to say that it failed at the first application because it seemed that people living in, and owning, a house together for any enterprise must be doing so to gain benefit from it, even if only free board and lodging. The establishment of a wider Board of Directors than just ourselves, and a commitment to pay rent, eventually got around this. But once more, a decision taken for one reason had wider implications. Wellspring's Board of Directors includes the "core" community of people with administrative responsibility for the enterprise. "Outside" members must always outnumber "inside" ones, however, to ensure accountability to the wider community, but the Board, working together through the years, operates as a group of friends, a phenomenon which surprises and even shocks people accustomed to a separated and even antagonistic Board-Staff relationship. This non-hierarchical and, in practice, consensus style of decision making has become an important indication and expression of Wellspring's values.)

In practice, the group did not wait for the occupancy permit to accept its first guest. By October that first year the little community was wondering whether anyone would ever come, and getting somewhat tired of each other's faces. On December 8th two people came. The first was Ellen, who has been part of Wellspring's life in one way or another ever since. A lifetime of living hand-to-mouth on the streets, lodging where she could when she could, had begun when her elderly and not very caring foster parents both died. After her foster-mother's death, she, a young teenager, had nursed her senile and incontinent foster-father, but on his death, found herself at sixteen with no home. (Her own mother had put her in foster care at ten days old, never released her for adoption, and seldom saw her.) Just before Ellen came to Wellspring she had a room in return for caring for an old man whose chief requirements were huge amounts of wine, so she slept with a knife in her bed, fearful of attack from her half crazy landlord. The house burned down when he set fire to his bed, and Ellen escaped with her life after vainly trying to save his. The Red Cross brought Ellen to Wellspring, and her photo appeared in the paper.

(This was the first of many articles in local papers about Wellspring: in this one the place was supposed to be inhabited solely by nuns — including, presumably, Paul!)

Ellen remembers to this day the exact spot in the kitchen on which she stood, clutching a plastic bag of donated clothes (she had lost all her own). The memory of that experience of fire traumatized her for years, but indeed her life experiences had already deprived her of health and a sense of any reality other than the need to survive. Funny, acute, loyal, self absorbed, hallucinating and yet present to people of all kinds, naive and yet suddenly maturely wise, Ellen confounds categories and taught us much — about what can be changed when no one believed change possible, and also what cannot be changed but must be lived differently.

With Ellen and with others, we began to test out what hospitality was all about. On the same day came Jane's younger sister, Veronica, victim of the same family situation, finally running after she had been beaten once too often. With a very different personality, her way of dealing with the past was different too. Lively, lovable, manipulative, full of dreams she lacked the self-knowledge to realize, always running, yet always longing for something better, she caused many heartaches during her time at Wellspring, and more since. She also taught us painful lessons about the limits of good will, about how change does and does not happen. Hospitality is not enough? Or is our definition of hospitality inadequate?

We talked of empowerment — giving people a chance to make a new life. What did it mean? Another of our earliest guests was a mother who suffered from multiple scelerosis, and her son aged four. (At this time we had not yet finished the extra rooms and therefore had no occupancy permit! We kept quiet and justified the inclusion of new guests by reminding each other that the occupancy permit was requested only for the new rooms, but the Inspector had said *we* could build on and live in anything we liked — so Nancy and I moved into the half-finished new rooms, and the mother and son went into the space we had vacated, while Ellen had the only other spare room and Veronica also moved into a new room, on the argument that she was Jane's sister and therefore "family" and one of us! To such casuistry does one resort, when dealing with the bureaucracy.)

Our assumption was that our attitude of welcoming acceptance and support would help a person whose life had been shattered to find healing, and space to begin to make some decisions for the future. Living with a woman whose troubles reached back beyond homelessness and her sickness to her childhood and failed marriage, we became aware that her chaotic way of life, her lack of parenting skills, were not going to change just because people were kind. At first some of us reacted by taking over and doing the parenting she lacked the energy and hopefulness to undertake, and by listening, caring, indulging. Far from being energized or taking any steps to reorder her life, she sank further into depression and chaos, and sat at the kitchen table waiting to die.

The manipulative behavior characteristic of people who have been abused and made dependent was new to us. Her social worker, the child psychologist who saw her son, and ourselves were kept apart, all hearing different stories, a strategy which enabled her to maintain herself in her depression and her dependence. Urged by Marygrace whose counseling experience was helpful in showing us what was going on and suggesting different approaches, eventually we asked for a case conference. We confronted what was happening. She heard different people saying the same things, we heard the psychologist's view of the child, and she knew we heard it. The game-playing stopped. She began to assume some parenting responsibility because we asked her to. She began to go to meetings of other MS sufferers, to take a more hopeful look at her life and make some plans. With help from Marygrace, limits were set, demands made, yet friendship, support and real concern were still present. The result was that the MS went into remission, her spirits improved and so did her energy. One of us advocated for her through the complex and frustrating process of obtaining disability benefits, and eventually she won them. Nine months after her arrival she found a new apartment, and Wellspring people helped to clean it and move in stored furniture. Years later, she and her son come back to Wellspring occasionally for holiday celebrations including "little" Mark's birthday. He is no longer little, but after all these years still feels a bond with Wellspring and the people he knew there. There is the hope that in his difficult home life the memory can make a difference, for their life is still chaotic. But the mother has maintained her sense of hopefulness. So, we at Wellspring were beginning to learn that love, support, "modelling" of good relationships or child care are important, but they are not enough.

They are not enough for people who may have experienced abuse since childhood, whose families have always been in debt, whose relationships have been insecure or alienating. They are not enough for troubled teenagers, or middle-aged women whose men have disappeared and left them unsupported, without jobs or job skills. They are not enough for people recovering from drugs or alcoholism or mental illness. They are not enough for the dispossessed who do not own themselves.

But if people come to the house with huge and longstanding problems, compounded by the homelessness which brings them to us, what are the chances of change? What can change the destructive patterns of a lifetime? That is the basic question which is posed for people trying to live out of the gospel proclamation. The gospel is about the possibility of transformation — what does that mean in practice? Does it happen, can it happen? In terms of individuals we serve, change is difficult, slow, easily undone, always fragile, sometimes, it seems, impossible. Does that mean Jesus was just fantasizing? Or does it mean that the things that make change so hard for individuals are wider than the individual? Are we dealing with the need for systemic change, not only personal change? Who is the problem — the homeless person, or the system (family, bureaucratic, religious) which did not help them? At what point can we intervene? Must we think in terms of response at several levels?

These are questions which now seem obvious, and we labor at the answers to some of them. Yet it took several years for the questions to become defined in a way that made it possible to begin to frame answers. Part of the purpose of this book is to show not only what the questions are but how one begins to ask them.

It took us four or five years to get to the point of formulating some answers, and therefore knowing what new questions to ask, and after nine years of hospitality the questions re-form and the answers are often elusive; nine years of something gradually surfacing which I can only call rage.

Nine years of opening your home to people in extreme need, nine years of living with them day and night. Nine years of learning that homelessness is the tip of the iceberg, the visible crisis which caps a thousand previous invisible crises of abuse, rejection, broken relationships, broken health, broken trust — which evoked no effective help. Nine years of working with guests to establish the fragile beginnings of self-respect and hope, to stimulate at least the desire to take a different road. Nine years of seeing many slide back into old patterns, make the same mistakes yet again that they and their parents and grandparents made, and that they are preparing their children to make also. Nine years of guests who have left, coming back to celebrate Thanksgiving or Passover, to tell us about successes (getting into school, a new job, a better relationship) or to ask for help in yet another crisis or sorrow. Nine years of learning — learning to live together, learning to part, learning to live with troubled people, learning to deal with agencies, government, public opinion. Nine full years, which have gradually led us to work on a theology and a spirituality that could enable us to engage these realities, to forge a methodology as well as a vision.

There was Diana who came with a little boy of two who had been in and out of hospital throughout his short life. He was unable to speak clearly and was found to be partially deaf. She came from a very disturbed family and from abusive relationships. In the weeks after they arrived the social worker who visited her tried to help her to play with the child, for like so many abused or neglected children she had no models in parenting, no sense of a child as a person, had never been played with herself or felt accepted as a human being. She had lost hope and confidence and her appearance showed it. Gradually her health and spirits improved, she began to be able to claim the right not to be abused. One day she was able to say, "I'm not going to let myself be treated like shit!" Yet, at least for the time, her new sense of self was not strong enough. She returned to the same relationship. Later she broke away again and managed to maintain a chaotic kind of independence, struggling to deal with a child who was often sick. She kept in contact with Wellspring, invited members to her home, eventually found a stable relationship, and continues to count on Wellspring as a source of help and support as she and her partner struggle to keep their home and (now) two children, with low paid jobs and rising rents.

Leonard was seventeen, without family, very disturbed and with an uncontrollable temper. He was a bed-wetter. He used and dealt drugs because that made him needed and gave him prestige among his peers, or so he thought. He was used and despised by the other kids whose friendship he longed for. He came to Wellspring malnourished, wild, having been sleeping in the woods, and struggled to make a fresh start, went into a training program, but was back in a week. He could not keep rules or his temper. He tried another program based in a home, went back to drugs, broke all the rules. He drifted away, called Wellspring once in a while, then disappeared.

Grace was twenty-seven, pregnant, neglected and rejected by older sisters who regarded her as the black sheep of the family, a role she learned to accept and play. Thrown out by the baby's father when her pregnancy became obvious, she came to Wellspring, and stayed until a few months after the baby's birth. It was a stormy relationship, yet a basis of trust was built up, even though we were, inevitably, often the enemy. Eventually she obtained a subsidized apartment after a great deal of hard work by the staff in calls and visits to the landlord, the Housing Authority, the Public Health department. Then a team cleaned down the apartment, helped her get furniture and move in. She could not keep to a budget, was always in debt, grumbled and complained, began counseling, and gave it up when it became confrontational. Yet the baby throve, growing up gentle, interested, secure. In the midst of muddle, the mother and child loved each other. A much younger man came on the scene and moved in, was cared for, spoiled. Selfish, jealous and demanding as he was, the craving to be needed was so deep that to respond to him seemed worth while. Through it all, Wellspring was a place to come back to, to help out, to celebrate, to fight with and grumble at, a solid rock to tie one's boat to in the ebb and flow of insolvency and emotional instability. There are desires for change that surface, an image of a different life, education, security, a better home, but there is so much in the way, for young women like this.

Who is the problem? The messed up kids from messed up families? That is the usual verdict. One response to this is to say: homelessness is a pathology. If you give them a new home, they will break it up, get in debt, be out again in six months. There is an obvious medical model to deal with it: if the poor are sick, they need treatment. They need to be institutionalized, put into mandatory programs to provide counseling, training in life skills, job training, parenting training. When we are through with them they should be useful members of society. Of course there isn't enough money to do that for more than a tiny number, and that's the pity; the rest will just have to muddle along. Their children will be taken into care if necessary, the parents may be imprisoned, or they may subsist on the street. The root of this attitude, implied in the "medical model" itself, is that the poor, being "sick", are not really citizens and need not be treated as responsible adults. They are, in other words, culturally enslaved; if they are "good" they may receive a limited kind of "freedom", contingent upon continuing to be "good"—that is, to display the appropriate servile virtues of obedience, patience, diligence, and submissiveness to authority. This is how patients in hospital are usually made to feel, this is how the "medical model" operates: by enslaving people "for their own good", but in reality for the profit of the ones with power.

However, we can use the medical model another way. There is such a thing as social pathology. We live in a society gripped with a fear amounting to paranoia — a fear of an "enemy" which is always waiting to attack us and take away the little bit we have managed to accumulate. For their own purposes, governments and corporations mystify the facts, feeding the fear and attaching it to some "outside" group or race. Changing with the times and the fashions, the enemy is Jews, Blacks, Communists, hippies. But consistently (and often combined with one or other of these labels) it is the poor. Of course, for purposes of propaganda, they are not referred to as poor, because that might arouse sympathy. Instead, they are the welfare-cheats, bums, junkies, sluts, layabouts, crazies. They are the people whose neediness is terrifying because it represents what might happen to us if something went wrong. Put that together with the fear of the "empire" over there, which so many continue to feel is still waiting to swallow us up, and you have a society prepared to accept a defense budget inflated beyond any rational explanation, and social services reduced to the point where a person on Welfare lives at 50% of the "official poverty level". A society which lives with, and acts out of, a fear without rational foundation is a sick society. In that case, in a sense the medical model is helpful. The poor, in such an interpretation, are the victims of collective criminal lunacy.

So maybe it is society at large, and not people like Diana, Grace and Leonard, which is the problem. These "little ones" are indeed often sick and disturbed. The situation is comparable to that of people living near a toxic waste dump which leaks. People become sick, some die. Is the problem these sick people (in which case we move them out of their homes and treat them medically) or is it those who dumped the chemicals, because that is a cheap way to dispose of them, refusing to acknowledge the risks and determined to cover up any "mistakes"? Seen in such terms, a "medical" model for interpreting poverty makes sense, but not the sense in which it is usually applied.

Then there is the moral approach. The poor are clearly bad. They are lazy, they want to be supported, they (the women at least) are sexually self-indulgent and immoral. For instance, women who get pregnant and have a baby can, at present, obtain welfare payments for themselves and their children, so long as they don't live with the baby's father. This regulation, it is said, destroys family life, splits up couples. The "moral" answer is to take away the welfare payments, because then the mother will be obliged (to avoid starvation) to stay with her husband, or boy-friend. This is known as "keeping families together". (The fact that the man may be abusive to the mother or the child or both, and that she may have originally left him for that reason, is irrelevant to this line of reasoning.)

Another bit of the moral approach is to say, the poor are spongers, they could get jobs if they liked. In some cases they could. At minimum wage, un-unionized, a woman might make a little more than she gets from Welfare; but if she goes off Welfare she loses her Medicaid, which secures some health care for herself and her children; she also has to pay for daycare if the employer doesn't provide it (and the waiting list for subsidized daycare is often years long). She may need a car to get to work at all, yet is unlikely to be able to afford even an old one.

The truth is that in America in the nineties you can have a full time job and still be poor, because big profits and big salaries for management and for the highly skilled depend on employing millions of people at wages which do not allow them to live decently, and in conditions which undermine their health and endanger their children, even if they can afford to rent at all. The major part of this huge labor force is women. These poor (employed or unemployed) are a problem created and sustained by political forces for economic reasons. The moral analysis of poverty, which understands that people are poor because they are lazy, unpatriotic, sexually immoral and self-indulgent (they have too many babies) needs to be turned on its head. There *is* a moral analysis, which understands that people are poor because others are greedy and power-hungry, indifferent to justice and compassion. The society is immoral and the poor are its necessary victims.

People like the staff at Wellspring, who spend their time working with the poor, need to keep in mind these common responses to the phenomenon of poverty, and experiment every now and then by taking the popular verdict and turning it inside out. We are all part of that sick and immoral society, and blaming the victim is easy. We all tend to do it, because the victims of oppression and abuse (political, economic or personal) are not always heroic characters. They are not martyrs for the cause, but often unhappy people whose experiences have made them suspicious and angry, and yet apathetic and dependent. Many have lost hope, but have learned some survival skills. They know how to manipulate, they know how to divide people, they know how to say and do the pleasing thing that will get them off the hook or get them what they want for the time being. They know how to evade, and stall, when to cry and when to threaten. Many, in fact, are indeed sick, and their values are warped. Most of all, in many cases the motivation to change is almost nil because they cannot clearly envision the advantages of such a huge undertaking.

This is not to deny that many are, in the clearest sense, heroic. There are young single mothers who get up at 5:30 to get the children to day care, and go on to work a full day, or to school. At the end of the working day they must find time to create a home, clean, shop, play with the children, and perhaps study after the children are in bed. They persevere, acquire qualifications, hold down jobs, bring up their children well. But those who can do this, through a combination of personal character and much support, really cannot be used as a standard to condemn those who do not manage to be like them. Poor education, poor health, and lack of supportive relationship can make it impossible even to dream of such an achievement.

This is the hardest thing for many who work with oppressed people. They come to realize that change is very hard, often virtually impossible at the level of individual lives. It is hard not only because the economic system is designed to keep a pool of poverty for its own purposes, but because poor people, in one sense, don't want to change. They want things to be a little better, they may even dream of a wonderfully different life, a life like the people in soap operas, but they can't or at any rate don't make an imaginative bridge between their present condition and any possible different reality.

The alternative moral interpretation of poverty, then, locates the sin in the values of an unjust society, just as the alternative "medical" model unexpectedly diagnoses the cause of sickness in a diseased social system, though its victims naturally are infected too. Neither interpretation gives the person of faith much encouragement. A strong conviction of the basic goodness of each person can become very theoretical as it is gradually eroded by the experience of the extreme toughness of the roots of destruction in the hearts and minds of abused and oppressed people, who have too often internalized the abuse and oppression and are busy abusing and oppressing themselves. The result of the split between conviction and experience, the day-long, yearlong, struggle to make real the things that *must* be true if there is to be hope for the world — this too often leads to burnout: disillusion, anxiety, displaced anger, cynicism, exhaustion, denial.

To deal with this, another interpretation of poverty has been developed. It is centuries old, though in our time it has been associated with the Catholic Worker movement especially. (This has to be qualified: the C.W. is enormously varied. Its "main-line" spirituality is not necessarily that of individual workers, and it is changing in many ways. But traditionally it is a spirituality of poverty, and it is very powerful.) The Catholic worker philosophy, among others, defines the Christian response to poverty as a call to immerse one's self in the life of the poor, to be friend and companion to those in need. A famous picture called "The Christ of the Homeless" shows Jesus huddled on a sidewalk together with a man and woman of the streets. It expresses very well this sense that we are called, primarily, simply to *be with* the poor. We may minister to basic needs for food, clothing, and shelter, but the more important gift is simply that of friendship, and presence. This includes political activism, particularly in peace work and support of unionization, which grows out of a very articulate sense of social justice, but it does not evaluate its work with individual poor in terms of the expectation of visible social change. It does not make claims on behalf of the poor, nor attempt to build a bridge towards a moment when they should "inherit the earth". It accepts the fact of dispossession, of the alienation of men and women from the land that is theirs, and it exposes the scandal by living it and refusing to hide it, but it does not confront it with an alternative vision except in a poetic and theoretical way. Basically, it is enough just to serve. This removes some of the stress, because the goals thus defined are achievable and to some extent satisfying. It is a way that requires a very strongly defined spirituality through which the experiences of poverty may be understood and assimilated. The presence across the nation of Catholic Worker houses, the hospitality they embody, the witness they give to the worthwhileness of even the most abandoned human being, is without price. It is a way to go, and it fills a great need both in the givers and receivers of service.

This is a spirituality, a way to live the terrible reality of poverty as a personal experience that can be life-giving, and it has a respectable history in the long procession of saints and heroes who, through the centuries, have dedicated themselves to the service of the poor, striving to see in the face of the leper or the beggar the face of Christ. This is a spirituality, but like all spirituality it has a theological basis, and if we look at it carefully this theological interpretation of poverty (like the usual medical and moral models of interpretation), tends to isolate the poor and treat poverty as a discrete phenomenon unrelated to its context. The medical model sees the poor as sick, the moral model sees them as sinful (unless we turn these two around, as I did earlier) and this theological model wraps the poor in a halo, perceiving them as especially the locus of God's blessing.

This theological model was very clearly expressed in 1986 by Cardinal Law of Boston when he celebrated a special Mass for the homeless on the feast of the Holy Cross, his Cathedral's pastoral feast. Present were many providers of shelter, and many homeless people. The theme of the homily was that the poor and homeless are especially blessed because they stand close to the cross, they share the redemptive suffering of Jesus. And those who provide shelter and food, said the Cardinal, are doing a necessary work, but must never forget that to provide for people's physical needs is not the most important thing. It is their spiritual needs that must come first.

Some of us walked out of that liturgy, yet in the light of the texts usually used to support such an interpretation, this seems like a well-founded bit of theologizing. Its basis is the theme of the "anawim", the poor remnant of Israel which, in the Hebrew scriptures, remains faithful in quiet hope, providing the little, insignificant but fertile vineyard where the word of God can be planted and take root. The poor are the special focus of the love and work of Jesus, his favorite companions, his particular care. He calls them, heals them, eats with them, calls them blessed, defines the coming reign of God as their natural habitat. The good news is proclaimed to the poor, they are the precious "little ones" whose treatment, good or bad, reflects attitudes to himself. There is no need to enumerate the texts, they are many and well known and clearly indicate that in the life and teaching of Jesus the poor have a very special role as the beloved children of the Abba. Jesus was passionate about the poor and this strand in his own feeling is probably the strongest and most characteristic.

In spite of all this, the Wellspring experience has not led those who shared it to feel satisfied with this particular theology of homelessness. The feeling among members did not change because people sat down with the texts of scripture and looked for an alternative, nor was the dissatisfaction expressed in words for a long time. Rather, a theological re-thinking was forced on us by a mounting uneasiness finally erupting into rage.

It is hard to reconstruct the stages of this corporate enragement, but some causes of questioning and disillusion stand out. One big one has been the experience of the curious little organism already referred to called "Movement for North American Mission", which was an essential element in the early Wellspring experience. As a hope and a dream it predated the beginning of Wellspring, and was conceived as a training program for Christian laypeople who felt called to serve the poor in their own country. The program was worked over and discussed over many months and eventually emerged as a two-year-plus experience, beginning with a very intense five-week orientation, based in the house at Wellspring, though trainees received bed and breakfast hospitality from friends in the city and neighborhood. This was followed by two full years of experience of working with poor people in a "deprived" area, rural or urban, with the support of two of us (Nancy and myself) as directors, plus local support from people experienced in the appropriate skills and knowledge. This was a tough and testing experience, it brought out unknown gifts but also raised hidden personal issues. It brought people mostly from middle class backgrounds into direct contact with the results of an unjust economic and social system, and this could be painful but also energizing.

The energizing bit, however, has not been the experience of all, and the reason why it has not is educational for us. References to those who worked in the program have already been made, and their stories will recur, for although the numbers were small and the program short-lived it attracted some remarkable people who remain in one way or another part of the Wellspring experience. (One, Mary Kay, who worked for two years in West Virginia later became part of the Wellspring staff, and another, Barbara, whose mission work was in the devastated city of Gary, Indiana, also worked as weekend staff.) But there were many who applied to the program, whose motivation for seeking a time of service of the poor would certainly not have stood up to the kind of experience the mission trainees underwent, and which indirectly taught us some clearer questions and answers.

The first hint of the problem occurred during initial formation weekends when interested people spent two days at Wellspring to learn about the program, and to be interviewed. We very soon discovered that, for some, service to the poor meant using the poor as a means to personal and spiritual fulfillment. Women dealing with the lingering humiliation and emptiness of the aftermath of divorce, men whose careers had been unsatisfying, adult children of alcoholics who had an obscure sense of inadequacy masked by religious language about humility, people who used spirituality as a way of not dealing with deep hurts in their past — these were the ones who told us they had a divine calling to serve the poor. As we talked we did not experience in such people any anger at injustice or abuse, nor much real understanding of what poverty does to people. Rather it seemed that "the poor" became the object of a quasi-romantic devotion which isolated its object from the rest of life and people, and in an odd way dehumanized those it claimed to serve. One woman admitted that she had no experience of poor people and was afraid of them — but she needed to "commit herself" to experience real vocation. Others seemed to have a real need to punish themselves, as if to "atone" for what they perceived as emotional failure. Some of these were themselves victims of abuse and rejection, and in some cases, of incest. In such people there was no sign of the energy of compassion which shows itself as appropriate anger, raising a need to understand the causes for the suffering of the poor, and to address the causes as well as the effects.

Yet, among those whom we accepted to enter into the full mission training program there were also some with painful personal experiences of alcoholic family, of rejection and self-doubt, and all of these naturally affected the ways they dealt with the people they encountered in their work. The difference was that they were willing to recognize the source of their pain, to work on their own issues and so avoid working out their pain on the people they served, by denying the roots of it. They found that, indeed, contact with suffering raised up old and terrible feelings, but when that happened they sought help and worked through it; they did not try to deny, to escape nor to spiritualize.

It was only with time and experience that we came to recognize quickly the mentality which uses the poor as emotional compensation for feelings of inadequacy while genuinely believing the poor are being served. This is a more subtle version of the idea that "charity" is the Christian duty of the well-to-do, and a wise Providence arranges for a supply of suitable objects (the "deserving" poor) in order that the souls of the rich may be saved. It is a horrible distortion of the gospel saying that "whatever you did to the least of my brothers and sisters, you did to me": we did it for God — not really for *them*!

In trying to understand, for ourselves, how our religious perceptions changed, how we became angry and determined people who strove to find a different language of religion because the old one would not do, it was important to see how a false attitude to the poor and to poverty, even in people of genuine good will, really contradicted the call we perceived in the gospel to sustain a vision of a different society, a society of justice and compassion in which "the meek inherit the earth."

The dilemma in which we were caught presented itself to us quite often in the context of a need (shared by all non-profit organizations with little assured income) to apply for grants for capital improvements, whether to private foundations or the State. A great deal of work goes into grant-writing and (as all the handbooks tell you) to have a chance of success the applicant must use the language of the granting body. It is necessary to express one's own aims and methods in terms of the aims and methods of the people who are going to read the application. In this context, writing accounts of the purpose of Wellspring can sometimes seem to require us to present ourselves as able and willing to recycle damaged human beings into acceptable citizens: wage-earning, independent, law-abiding, paying taxes instead of being supported by them. As we write and discuss this kind of stuff we grow angry.

Sometimes it feels as if we are being co-opted, at least seeming to agree with the oppressive system. It is as if we also were saying that the poor are the problem, but it (they) can be fixed. However, it is not even that simple; behind the corporate "bodies" we address are real bodies, humans, and when a few are actually encountered we discover compassionate people who rejoice that a few of those hurt by economic "fate" can be helped, and who want to support efforts to do so. There is a real, and often religious, belief that the political and economic system is basically beneficial to all, that everyone can eventually "make it", with hard work and help, and that therefore what Wellspring and other similar groups are doing, and grantors and donors are supporting, is to befriend those accidentally hurt by unfortunate side-effects of a system otherwise 'sound'.

Fortunately, and significantly, this is not the whole story. One of the encouraging things is to discover that even among grant-making bodies there are some, especially those created by women and some churches, which came into being, it seems, out of an awareness that re-cycling damaged human beings is not what we need to be about, but that basic social change is needed. This helps us to keep our own values from being dimmed by the fog of false public expectations.

The dilemma is that on the one hand we are aware of, and want to act out of, the fact that poor people are the victims of an economic and social situation they did not create, but on the other hand if they are to "make it" in the sense they themselves understand it they must fit themselves to the expected mould. To survive financially and even emotionally they must learn to work the system. Also, "the system" is inside them. They value themselves according to the standards imposed on them by those who have made it impossible for them to reach those standards. So it feels as if we are — and in some sense we really are — helping to perpetuate the values that produce oppression.

For instance, a young single woman is moving out into her own home; she has three hundred dollars saved after her time at Wellspring; that won't buy much furniture but with gifts and some second-hand pieces one can manage. But for her the idea of friends visiting and seeing second-hand furniture is a disgrace, and she may break her carefully developed budget and borrow from friends or buy on credit to have the new couch and color TV which, to her, represent self-respect. So at the price of financial anxiety and deprivation, she does indeed feel good, and so we rejoice with her, knowing how important this is to her, but also how she is really being exploited.

When a woman gets a scholarship to college, or gets a job that will just get her off Welfare, it is right to rejoice, yet these successes may simply embed her at a different level in the system that will always pay her less than a man for the same work. (The current statistic is that, overall, women are paid 60% of male earnings, at every level.) Women who, because they cannot get daycare, or haven't a car, or lack skills, cannot get a job or go to school, feel that they are failures as human beings, and everything re-enforces this, whether it is the attitude of the Welfare worker, or the landlord who won't rent to "subsidized" tenants, or the need to turn to the local Food Pantry when the children are hungry, or every night watching images of success on TV.

So, when a woman manages her little bit of success do we celebrate — or preach, instead, the beauty of poverty? Sometimes it can seem that helping a woman to "manage", as she must to survive, on very little, is somehow to confirm her feeling — and society's — that she isn't worth much anyway. Isn't that in a sense a tacit acceptance of society's verdict on the poor, that they are meant to be that way because they are basically "different" and inadequate? Simply to redefine inadequacy, and glorify it, is not the answer. It doesn't help the angry woman who slides yet again into drinking because, in middle-age, she is divorced, has no up-to-date job skills, and goes through interview after interview ending in further rejection and loss of hope. It doesn't help the young mother whose whole education has been in dependence on and manipulation of men, and whose self-respect is gone because in the event she has failed to "keep" one.

And it doesn't help us, as women living with other women, trying to understand our own situation in relation to the system that certainly enables us to earn our living by providing shelter to other women, but does so on the tacit understanding that we will play the game that poor women can never win. And the way out through a spirituality that embraces poverty as a good is not for us. The alternative became clear to us very directly through reading the gospels, combined with some basic social analysis.

We did this together with our mission trainees (the ones who were not looking merely for spiritual justification or escape). With these some of us spent five weeks reading the gospel of Mark in daily sections. At the same time the trainees were seeing short films on aspects of the economy of poverty, they were listening to invited speakers, they were reading assigned books, and they were experiencing the small city of Gloucester itself as a laboratory in which to test out the economic, political and religious insights they were discovering. They talked to sailors in bars, bag ladies on benches, to police, City Councilors, social workers, teachers, teenagers. They heard different points of view about unemployment, alcohol, welfare, crime, education. We showed them films about the methods and values of international corporations, and the workings of the welfare system. And every day we read part of Mark's gospel.

The gospel became the touchstone by which to evaluate feelings and experiences. The outrage and frustration, the admiration and compassion, raised by encounters with the reality of poverty, and the first insights into the causes of it, were rediscovered and transformed by the shared study of the gospel. For the first time some began not only to revere the Man from Nazareth as Savior, but to understand him as a person moved by emotions they could share. They could share the feelings because they shared the experiences of seeing the reality and the effects of poverty, and like him they could perceive also the reasons for it in an accepted system based on the dispossession of some so that others might possess more.

For some of the mission trainees that was a shattering experience. Precious images of Jesus were tarnished. The awesome yet comforting spiritual support, the God untouched by real human feelings, the a-political benefactor and lover of the weak — these "Jesuses" were challenged, and threatened to disappear. One woman wailed, "You are taking Christ away from me!", for the person with whom they were all becoming acquainted as we read Mark's gospel was too human, too vulnerable, too angry. He could not provide a validation for the acceptance of suffering and humiliation because he was seen to be attacking by word and deed a religious system that did just that. It validated suffering and poverty because, like most religious systems, it knew them as "God's will", and so it maintained its control over the poor (poverty or sickness being the result of sin) and so had to atone by giving to God, through God's self-appointed representatives. (In our time money pours in to the bank accounts — and expense accounts — of TV evangelists, and most of it comes from the poor, for exactly the same reason as, two thousand years ago, the widow put "all she had" into the Temple collection box. Far from praising this generosity, Jesus was enraged that the system, created by people who had "plenty", extracted from the poor their "all".)

For some of our trainees, when these realities finally became clear, the result was a revolution. The compassion which had motivated their decision to join the mission program found new and deeper roots, and issued in a new clarity about the purposes of mission, the nature of vocation and the meaning of the "good news". It was a personal and inner revolution, but one made possible in the community of shared search, prayer, discussion, discovery. It was a painful experience but for them an energizing one, and it carried some of them forward into two years of working with marginalized people, with a whole new understanding of what they themselves were about and of the meaning of God and of church.

The discovery made in five weeks of intense, many-leveled work by the mission trainees was one shared by the Wellspring community and developed and deepened over a long period. It was, as indicated earlier, this study of the gospels which motivated the group from which Wellspring emerged, but the experience of living there pushed us to reflect again, to work at more deeply searching questions around the texts we thought we understood.

The radicalizing process is complex and ongoing. It is fueled by many things. Obscure dissatisfaction growing to anger at some of the attitudes of human service agencies and churches is one aspect of it, but the deepest questions arose from the gradual discovery of the danger of our own co-option, of the fact that, over and over, we found ourselves drawn into trying to impose middle-class values and points of view on people who had been damaged by the side effects of those very things, but then pulling back and questioning ourselves.

We began to see that the Jesus of the synoptic gospels was affirming the experiences of the marginalized of his time as valid and normative openings to a different future. Blessed are the poor, the mourners, the hungry, the unjustly persecuted, because the will of the Abba is that they become part of a very different experience. Jesus validated his own mission, to the emissaries of John the Baptist in prison, by reference to the prophecies of a transformed society precisely for those people who were damaged by the sins of the present age. "Go and tell John what you have seen and heard; how the blind recover their sight, the lame walk, the lepers are made clean, the deaf hear, the dead are raised to life, and the poor are hearing the good news." The proclamation of a transformed world echoed Isaiah, and the passage quoted from the prophet goes on, interestingly, to see as the place of all this human healing and new life a land in which the wildernesses blossom, dry places bubble with springs and grow green. This is the place where a "causeway" will be built for God's people to come home to their own land.

When women are obliged to go to the Welfare system for help they often encounter contempt, condemnation, long delays, and even refusals of the benefits to which they are legally entitled. In reaction to these usual attitudes the women are often angry, they make scenes, cry, swear, storm out, which provides a further excuse to deny them services. Or they are incoherent, don't provide necessary information because they are too confused, and give up at the first rebuff. From the middle-class point of view, it is obvious that these kinds of reaction are counter-productive. One should go to the Welfare Office in a cooperative frame of mind, with all necessary documents and clear answers. One must bite one's tongue in response to off-handed rudeness, be patient, if necessary ask to speak to a high authority, and remain throughout unflustered, smiling and calm. All this, besides being quite impossible for a person in the throes of personal crisis, is a tacit admission that the system is just and that its attitude to the poor is justified, when we know very well that neither is true. (The fact that some Welfare workers are courteous, compassionate people, trying to humanize an unjust, paper-laden bureaucracy over which they have no control, does not alter the system. There are heroines and heroes within it, but the thing is by its nature oppressive.)

It is part of our job to advocate for the poor in such circumstances, precisely because the detached and confident middle-class persona is acceptable and gets results and even politeness. The very same people who feel licensed to scream at the poor that they have no right to ask the tax payer to make up for their laziness and lack of foresight speak with gentle reasonableness to the middle-class advocate. So to do good advocacy, and obtain the benefits to which the poor are legally entitled, we are obliged at least to appear to render to Caesar what is God's — that is, the power to forgive and redeem.

Where, in the light of the gospel, does a possible way forward show itself? How can we avoid the horns of the dilemma — on the one hand the danger of co-option by the system whose victims we claim to serve, or on the other hand the impossibility of total disengagement from the system, if we are to support our guests in the only means open to them to survive and lay the foundations of a different future?

Our conclusion, reached painfully and still to be explored and fully lived, comes to us in the discovery of the nature of the prophetic as we encounter it in the personality and mission of Jesus.

This theological exploration did not, as it might seem, emerge in some separate religious area of our lives in which we reflected on Scripture and then tried to apply it to everyday attitudes and decisions. The concern and the anger and the confusion emerged, for instance, especially during weekly staff meetings, when we review the needs and progress of each guest. At this time the person who is working one-on-one with a particular guest gives a summary of the week's events and gets feed-back from other staff. Not only the pain and problems of the guests emerge, but the doubts and questioning of the staff team, and these concerns are raised explicitly at times of shared "supervision" when the staff team takes time to reflect on its own reactions, methods, and underlying questions. At these times the issues are not necessarily raised in theological form, but these same issues are raised in the context of readings (from Scripture and other sources) chosen to be shared each Sunday, as well as at more informal times. There have been many times when the paradox of the work which tries to be empowering, and is yet confined and distorted by its cultural context, has come through with such force that people have wept openly. So to say that a way forward seems to open through understanding the nature of the prophetic work and function is to say that a whole experience of life was brought to a kind of focus by this concept. It does not mean that the religious symbol made everything clear, or somehow "sanctified" an otherwise unchanged reality. There is an ongoing dialectic, in which new questions are opened up and new answers require changed responses which generate yet more questions.

A formative influence for us as a group was Walter Brueggemann's book, "Prophetic Imagination", for it made clear to us the twin tasks of the prophet, as they are shown in the Hebrew Scriptures, as Jesus lived them, and as the followers of that Way are called to live them. These twin tasks of the prophet are those of denouncing and grieving, and of announcing and energizing. They are then holistic tasks, they demand energy of mind, heart, speech, action. One calls us to perceive and analyze what is wrong, to make it evident and known, by writing and talking about it, by protests and petitions, by any kind of personal, communal or political action. It calls us to rage and grieve and feel compassion. It calls us to be in solidarity with those who are hurt, giving practical help but also refusing to cover up what is wrong by pretending that by giving immediate help we are undoing the evil. The other calls us to have a vision of a different possibility and to support each other in holding fast to that and making it concrete and realizable. It calls us to believe in the transforming power of love in each person, to which Jesus appealed in order to set them free, and to know that this power can indeed create a different world where God is free to be the Abba of Jesus.

As months and years went by, as we struggled with the failure of what is usually called "church" to be prophetic, and as we worked through our own failures to be church and to be prophetic, the whole concept became central to us. It clarified our sense of what we are about, it relieved some of the guilt and frustration, it gave anger a direction and a transforming power.

The true depth and power of prophetic anger doesn't come easily. Because we are white and because we have learned all too well that anger is bad and dangerous, and because we are very much afraid to discover the depths even of our personal anger, let alone the anger of gender and class, we don't easily identify with such pure anger and longing for revenge as that quoted by Alice Walker in her book "In Search of Our Mother's Gardens". It is a "curse prayer", collected in the 1920's by Zora Neale Hurston and it is the kind of thing the prophets of Israel would have uttered without inhibition. Here, now, feeling often the prophetic impulse, we can at least remind ourselves that this is how oppressed people can feel, and appropriately feel; and this is how the prophetic rage can be concretized. As we read it we can realize that this prayer is, in fact, in danger of being granted, not by some external act of a separated deity but by the inward inexorable workings of the destructive power which is unleashed when human and earthly and heavenly wisdom, sweet and strong interdependence of all things, is violated. Then, things fall apart, dry up and are blown away. The water and air become foul, people and animals and fields become sterile, and Mother Gaia dies with those who caused her death, as they have caused the deaths of other women. The curse prayer calls on the Man God, the only God known to the praying one, but in truth the Man God is also a prophetic one who knew rage and knew what happens to the poor and to women as a blasphemy and the seed of destruction.

> "To the Man God: O Great One, I have been sorely tried by my enemies and have been blasphemed and lied against. My good thoughts and my honest actions have been turned to bad actions and dishonest ideas. My home has been disrespected, my children have been cursed and ill-treated. My dear ones have been backbitten and their virtue questioned. O Man

God, I beg that this that I ask for my enemies shall come to pass. That the South wind shall scorch their bodies and make them wither and shall not be tempered to them. That the North wind shall freeze their blood and numb their muscles and that it shall not be tempered to them. That the West wind shall blow away their life's breath and will not leave their hair grow, and that their fingernails shall fall off and their bones shall crumble. That the East wind shall make their minds grow dark, their insight shall fail and their seed dry up so that they shall not multiply.

"I ask that their fathers and mothers from their furthest generation will not intercede for them before the great throne, and the wombs of their women shall not bear fruit except for strangers, and that they shall become extinct. I pray that the children who may come shall be weak of mind and paralyzed of limb and that they themselves shall curse them in their turn for ever turning the breath of life into their bodies. I pray that disease and death shall be forever with them and that their worldly goods shall not prosper, their sheep, and their hogs and all their living beasts shall die of starvation and thirst. I pray that their houses shall be unroofed and that the rain, the thunder and lightning shall find the innermost recesses of their home and that the foundation shall crumble and the floods tear it asunder. I pray that the sun shall not shed its rays on them in benevolence, but instead it shall beat down on them and burn them and destroy them. I pray that the moon shall not give them peace, but instead shall deride them and decry them and cause their minds to shrivel. I pray that their friends shall betray them and cause them loss of power, of gold and silver, and that their enemies shall smite them until they beg for mercy which shall not be given them. I pray their tongue shall forget how to speak in sweet words, and that it shall be paralyzed and that all about them will be desolation, pestilence and death. O Man God, I ask you for all these things because they have dragged me in the dust and destroyed my good name; broken my heart and caused me to curse the day I was born. So be it."

This is a prayer of truth, but not the whole truth. As Alice Walter herself concludes at the end of the essay in which she quotes the curse prayer, ultimately we cannot identify ourselves with the results of that prayer, because it means the death not only of the destroyer but of all. At moments that can seem worth the cost, but it isn't. "And with this knowledge," she writes, "it becomes increasingly difficult to embrace the thought of extinction purely for the assumed satisfaction of — from the grave — achieving revenge. Life is better than death, if only because it is less boring, and because it has fresh peaches in it."

This is a very prophetic statement; the prophets of Israel had a strong feeling that eating fruit was what God wanted people to be able to do, only the fruit was for everyone, including the people who grow it. And so the other prophetic task is actually a lot harder but — and this has to be constantly remembered — cannot be undertaken unless the task of rage and grief has first been fully lived. The other task is that of affirming the possibility of eating peaches. Peaches grow on trees, and trees grow in land. Ultimately the affirmation of newness is the affirmation of land — land for the dispossessed, the people who grow peaches and never get to eat them. As Alice Walker says, "In any case, Earth is my home — though for centuries white people have tried to convince me I have no right to exist, except in the dirtiest, darkest corners of the globe. So let me tell you: I intend to protect my home. Praying — not a curse — only the hope that my courage will not fail my love. But if by some miracle, and all our struggle, the earth is spared, only justice to every living thing (and everything alive) will save humankind.

"And we are not saved yet.
Only justice can stop a curse."

This is the prophetic voice, fierce and compassionate and passionate for justice. You can call it — it really is — "spirituality", and understood rightly that means one's life finds a different kind of meaning and direction. We can call it "prophetic spirituality", but that is not what people mean when they ask us, "what do you do about your spiritual lives?", as if spiritual life were something we could add on to our other activities in order to sanctify them and keep ourselves going. By it we mean that our life, with all its ups and downs, its uproar and its quiet times, its political aspect and its intense personal encounters, *is* our spirituality, and that it is about grieving and rejoicing, about forgiving, and hoping, and finally and eventually about land.

It is about *land*, about who has title to it, who, therefore, is "at home" in it. The prophets had much to say about the people in the land, about what was and what could be. The whole messianic vision was concerned with the possibility of a time and place of peace and plenty. The messianic banquet, which the Christian eucharist is intended to prophesy and somehow express, is about the creation of a community of shared bounty nurtured by the abundant breasts of God. The fertile land not only expresses but *is* the compassion of God, and it is for all. The power of the spirit gives God's life, in the land which is the gift of that same life-giving spirit, and the power fills people to enable them to claim what the prophets saw and promised. The Spirit of God empowers the exiles to undertake the long journey home.

Empowerment. The way out of the poverty trap. The recovery of hope and self-respect. The glimpse of a different world which is *home*. Empowerment is a wonderful word, but what does it mean in practice? Is it enough to help people achieve the only goals they easily perceive? As one woman put it, "I want a home of my own, a man I can respect, time with my children." Setting aside the difficulty of reaching even these apparently modest goals — is this all that empowerment is about? Even to find and afford and sustain a home is itself such a struggle and takes so much energy, support, and hard work that to look for anything more seems unrealistic. And men worthy of respect because they are capable of respect do exist but are not easily found in a society that admires Rambo and sustains a pornographic trade only slightly less lucrative than the drug traffic.

It takes a lot of "empowering", in a sense, to give a person who has lived always as a victim the conviction that she is capable of making choices even of the most practical kind. But that cannot be enough, overall. It may be all that some can reach to, at least for a time, but it leaves the wider situation, the reasons *why* simple goals are too difficult to attain, untouched and unchallenged. It even reinforces the oppressive system because it seems to prove that people *can* make a reasonable life for themselves if they accept the existing system and operate by its values. And it is true that some can do so even in a highly competitive situation. Some *will* win the race. But the nature of a race is that more lose than win.

The Gospel message is that this is not enough. Some of the people whom Jesus healed and liberated returned to their existing jobs and homes, but they were changed; they were not expected to "fit back into" the system that had subjected them to poverty, guilt and sickness. Perhaps some changed their home situation from within, and created those centers of vitality, vision and hope which later became known as "house churches", but many did not go back to their jobs and homes. They committed themselves to the work of prophetic proclamation. They became followers and their lives were changed in very visible ways. They were empowered, caught by a vision of a different possibility and wanting to make it happen. Prophetic spirituality is about that kind of empowerment, and at Wellspring we have tried to live that, with all the ups and downs and doubts and fears and hopes that are associated with the notion of "prophet".

One of the biggest obstacles to the prophetic task that we discovered is the numbness that enfolds people when they are deeply convinced that change — personal or communal — is not possible or even *right*. Because this is so deep in our culture and our religious consciousness it needs a chapter to itself, for at the heart of injustice is the conviction (in both oppressor and oppressed) that poverty and suffering are God's will.

CHAPTER FOUR
THE WILL OF GOD

Religion of a certain kind, which Marx described accurately as the "opium of the people" is as addictive and as destructive as other drugs on the market. It is sold openly and legally and carries no penalties for the pusher. Here is a story about how God's will is known:

A young woman came to Wellspring from the psychiatric ward of the local hospital. Requests for a place for people leaving hospital, and especially the psychiatric ward, are not uncommon. People who are, and have been, mentally sick face a huge handicap in finding a place to live, beyond all the problems the poor always face, and staff or volunteers doing telephone intakes at Wellspring hear stories of patients abandoned by relatives, jobless, without income, about to be discharged. "Can you take her (or him) 'for a few days'?" It really means. "Please take this person off our hands because we don't know what to do."

This particular young woman, whom I will call Barbara, had been in the hospital before. As a child she had been the victim of incest by her stepfather for some years but dared not tell her mother. It was only when, as a teenager, she discovered that her two younger sisters were also being abused that she decided to confide in a teacher at school. The teacher, understandably but unwisely, encouraged her to tell her mother. Before doing this Barbara talked to her younger sisters, who admitted the incest and promised to back her up when she spoke to their mother. But when she did so her mother utterly refused to believe her, and when Barbara appealed to her sisters for support they were too afraid to persist and denied what they had told her. The whole family turned on Barbara and accused her of lying, and when she persisted finally had her admitted to hospital as the victim of delusions. The shock of this experience was so great that for a while she retreated totally into herself, convinced that she must indeed be crazy, if memories that were so real could be denied by the people she had loved and trusted. But something inside her would not accept this verdict, insisted that she was sane and truthful. Gradually she reclaimed the outside world, but when she left hospital she was very much alone, still unbelieved and rejected. She began drinking, then quickly married, to find companionship and support, but experienced (predictably) further abuse and rejection. During this period also she was raped in the city one night, but she was able to tell the story very clearly.

Before her marriage broke up she became pregnant and had a little girl on whom her whole desire to love and be loved became focussed. But the strain had been too much: a few weeks later she broke down again and was admitted to hospital, and the baby was put into foster care. During her time of recovery she began to make toys and other gifts for her child, dreaming of the time when they would be reunited. It was after this time in hospital that she came to Wellspring. Still very fragile, she appreciated the care and support she received, and she talked constantly of her baby, and of her hopes — yet she could not resist her husband's continued demands that she visit him, and sexual experiences with him raised once more all the old fears and confusions so that she had to go back to hospital for a short time. It was after this that she became close to members of a local church, one of whom she had met while in hospital. Religion offered comfort, a sense of acceptance in spite of everything, friendship and meaning. She went to Bible study classes which gave her a social as well as a religious context, and the whole church experience made her feel happier than she had ever been.

However, the future of the baby was still undecided. Barbara, though better, was clearly not stable enough to make a home for her child, and would not be for some time, perhaps years. Should the child continue in foster care, with the hope of eventual reunion, or should she be freed for adoption? This was the agonizing choice that Barbara was asked to make. Her whole sense of the meaning of love had been focussed on this baby, yet she knew that it might be better for this child to go at once to a secure and permanent family than to wait and have to make the difficult adjustment later to her real but "new" mother.

In her indecision and grief Barbara consulted the pastor of her church. Which way was the will of God? How could she discover it?

Barbara had a limited period (some weeks) within which to make the decision. She was required to reach a decision and present it to the court on a certain date; if she asked to keep the baby the court would decide whether and when to grant her request. If, however, she made no decision, the court would make one for her.

The advice given by the pastor was interesting. Since she found it so hard to make a decision she was advised *not to make one*. She should leave it to the court, and whatever decision the court made would be known to be God's will.

Thus, this woman who had already been deprived of childhood, of sexual identity, of home, of family, and almost of sanity, was advised to give up that last stronghold of human integrity, the power of choice. Not to choose would absolve her of responsibility, would allow her to cradle herself in a God who demanded nothing and rewarded passivity. She was already, like all victims of incest, inclined to regard herself as a bad person, and this kind of religious attitude reinforced that, but gave her the chance to "atone" by giving up herself, accepting whatever came, however painful, as God's will and therefore "good" for her. Non-decision meant, almost certainly, losing her baby, and that would be a "punishment" her sins deserved — this at least was her feeling.

Something inherently healthy in this girl, the same something which had precariously preserved her sanity, caused her to refuse the advice. She made her own painful decision to give up her child for the child's sake. It was almost too much for her. Admitted to a rehabilitation program, she was happy at first, then ran away, began drinking again, but then went back. Wounded, she continues to struggle and grow. But that is not what a certain kind of spirituality envisions.

The will of God has been used, perhaps more than any other religious concept, to keep people without choices, but especially to keep women without choices. It is truly extraordinary how common it has been throughout Christian history for otherwise intelligent and gifted women to believe that it was required of them to give up their own sense of direction, to submit to situations and thoughts and actions which violated their integrity and common sense, because someone said, "it is the will of God." They hardly ever said, "How do you know?" (If they did they were no doubt punished or excluded, and not heard from again.) To learn to accept the inevitable with courage and hope is one thing: it is quite another to make something "inevitable" which is not, and to do so in God's name. Yet, in practice, our whole social system, past and present, is based on persuading huge numbers of people that it is fore-ordained (fate, God's will) that they be poor and inferior, and support by their labor and poverty the comfort and wealth of their superiors. All this is very familiar from the past: we no longer talk in those terms so openly. Most of us dare not actually say (unless we are fundamentalists) that God has decided that some are to be rich and some poor. But the sense that God rewards goodness with prosperity did not die out with the Puritans, or perhaps simply the Puritans are still with us. The converse of that is that those who do not prosper are not good, which is part of the underpinning of the "moral" interpretation of poverty: the poor are "bad".

The will of God as a kind of arbitrary magic to be discerned in events passively accepted is one kind of theology. It has a long history. It touches on a similar doctrine by which difficult decisions have been made by picking a Bible text after opening the book at random. At least, in such a case, the idea is that the text found will give guidance about making a choice; a little like the now popular use of the I Ching. The Bible, or some other source of wisdom, becomes an oracle. Because of the psychic involvement of the person who does this it actually works quite well in many cases. It does not make a virtue of passivity. The will-of-God-as-acceptance-of-circumstance theology is different and insidious because it is so close to the real heroism of those who do make a life out of almost intolerable circumstances, and even find occasions to rejoice and hope.

An example that springs to mind is the life of the Jewish *shtetl* in prerevolutionary Russia as described in a book by Sholem Alaichem and made into the musical, "Fiddler on the Roof." The characters in the story are desperately poor, and insecure even in their poverty (they are subject to arbitrary Czarist pogroms), but they have a tenacious will to survive and to enjoy themselves whenever possible, expressed in the lines of the wonderful song, "To Life", when the village men celebrate a wedding in prospect. "God wants us to be joyful even when our hearts are panting on the floor. How much more should we be joyful when there's really something to be joyful for!" So although it "has a way of confusing us, blessing and bruising us", they drink "to life." They cope with their very hard life, but not with passive submission. Their faith is one of vision and hope, even though distant, and this leads to a sense of inventiveness and adventure, demonstrated by the three daughters who in different ways break the precious mould of "tradition", which holds the fabric of their fragile society together. But this "tradition" is rooted in a theology of hope, not of passivity or guilt. When, in the end, they are forced to leave the only place they have ever known, one boy asks the Rabbi, "We have been waiting for the Messiah all our lives; wouldn't this be a good time for Him to come?" But the Rabbi replies, "We shall have to wait for Him somewhere else." Hope deferred is, with wry humor, still hope. They will make a new life because acceptance of the inevitable does not attribute it to God, but still looks to a God of freedom, the God of the Exodus, the God of the Return.

The passive submission encouraged by a theology of guilt does not breed hope, it leads to apathy and cynicism and the suppressed, unacknowledged anger which issues in such things as alcoholism, child abuse, depression and mental illness.

There is another form of the will-of-God-discovered-in-circumstances, theology which is based on the idea that one may be sure that one is acceptable to God and doing His will (it had to be *His*) by the benefits He bestows. One of the precious memories at Wellspring concerns an elderly lady called Edith. She has already been referred to briefly, and she came to Wellspring escaping from twelve years of physical and emotional abuse. She had been in a disastrous second marriage, after a previous long and happy marriage ending in her husband's death in an accident. It was this earlier marriage, plus memories of strong family love before that, which gave Edith the strength eventually to break out of the abusive second marriage and make a new life. Edith was a delight to have in the house. She was energetic, determined and interested in everything. She appreciated enormously small acts of kindness; when she had a cold and Mary Jane brought her a glass of orange juice in bed she wept — there had been no acts of kindness for many years. She loved everyone in the house but also tried to raise standards of housekeeping to her level of German meticulousness, and had a hard time living with younger women in the house who, she felt, showed a lamentable lack of discipline and order. With help and her own indomitable spirit she was able to find an apartment. With police escort and assistance from Wellspring people she reclaimed her own possessions from her old home and furnished her new one. (She knew *exactly* where each thing was to go, so in the face of our disbelief she managed to fit everything into a space less than half the size of her former home.)

As Edith's fortunes improved, and she began to look forward to a new life, her thankfulness to God was very great. She interpreted each beneficial change as evidence of God's care for her, and felt grateful and happy in that knowledge.

Edith affirmed and reaffirmed that the blessing of her restored happiness was proof of God's love for her. Once, someone at Wellspring asked her whether, if that were so, she felt that lack of good things in a person's life meant that she or he was not loved by God. She could not really make sense of this.

Religious people are taught to be thankful for good times as evidence of the love and mercy of God, and indeed this whole tradition, in every religious culture, of harvest festivals and all kinds of personal and communal celebrations is rooted in the sense that good things are somehow from God. The reverse side of this is the sense that bad things must be either a punishment, or a trial of faith, or perhaps evidence of the still unresolved struggle of good and evil, of God and anti-God. It did not occur to Edith that when she insisted that her changed fortune was evidence of God's care for her she was implicitly saying that God did not care for others whose fortunes remained bad, and even that God had not cared for her in her bad times. However, Edith was certainly never tempted to feel that God rewarded or wanted passivity. Although she endured twelve years of abuse before breaking free that was because her strong will and hopeful attitude made it seem possible for a long time that she could change the situation. It was only when she finally had to admit that it could not be changed that she left, and did so carefully and with planning and deliberation. She *decided* to leave in the fullest sense. In contrast, another elderly woman who stayed with us had remained in an abusive situation for forty years because she internalized (with help from her minister, friends and family) the idea that the good and holy thing was to submit, and to pray for change, not to initiate it. Her theology was of the acceptance-of-circumstance-as-God's-will variety. In the end hers was a purposefulness born of despair. She could no longer believe in the religious rationale nor in the possibility of change in her husband, and she left, with courage but with shattered health.

A younger woman at Wellspring who with her children had escaped from a psychotic and very abusive husband was once asked by a religious person whether she felt that the failure of her marriage might have been due to the fact that she had not prayed enough. Versions of this have been common spiritual currency in religious dealings with women for centuries; and indeed are closely related to the almost universal view that if a woman suffers abuse (including rape) it is her own fault. For women with a religious background such guilt-creating suggestions are very difficult to resist. The feeling of inferiority which has been part of their whole cultural conditioning and life experience is reinforced by the religious training which tells them that goodness, for a woman, means fidelity in marriage at no matter what cost, and that if the marriage is unsatisfactory and the husband abusive it is the woman's fault. The priest or minister or even counselor will ask, "What did you do to upset him?" and advise patience and cheerfulness and renewed efforts to please. When there has also been an earlier experience of incest the ability to feel one has any value at all as a person is almost nil. The result of all this is something we have seen over and over again at Wellspring. Women from religious homes whose marriages have failed feel themselves outcasts from God. They do not go to church nor do they want to join the informal liturgies of the house, because they feel (and even say) "I'm not good enough." They hear a verdict of exclusion from God and do not dispute it. This feeling is so deeply rooted, and so entwined with the other forces which make women feel bad, that it shapes all their choices or lack of choices. It is at least a major part of the reasons why women drift from one bad sexual relationship to another. They are convinced no "good man" would want them, and also that they *deserve* abuse and neglect. They distrust other women and turn from supportive women friends to unsupportive males because, at bottom, other women are as "bad" as themselves. They bring up their daughters to expect rejection and abuse (and often reject them emotionally at an early age) and their sons to expect service, privilege and non-accountability for their actions.

It seems clear that the theology of the will of God has been developed in such a way as to establish and maintain the power of the rich over the poor, of men over women, of white over black. In the ways indicated from the examples I quoted, it is used to enjoin passive acceptance of injustice, to deprive people of the power of choice and to create a sense of guilt which deprives them of the will to challenge or change their circumstances. None of this is a new idea. Anti-religious writers and polemecists have been saying this kind of thing for generations. My reason for saying it here is that the direct and daily experience of how this kind of theology shapes people's lives has forced us at Wellspring to re-examine our own theology and to critique it from a faith viewpoint, rather than an anti-faith one.

The history of Wellspring's "Movement for North American Mission" is again interesting here because it is the story of people wrestling with these issues. In the four years of its operation, these groups of people went through the five-week orientation and went on to spend two years in mission experience in some area of acute deprivation, not abroad but in their own country. There were, in the end, only twelve who undertook this two-year mission, and all of their stories are remarkable, though I can only touch on a few of them here.

They came from fairly traditional Christian backgrounds. They came because they were, as we saw earlier, looking for something different. Deep changes in attitude and awareness took place during the orientation, but it was the two years of mission that really broke open old categories and left them, vulnerable and sometimes almost despairing, to rebuild a sense of meaning. Two, Elaine and Barbara, began their experience under the auspices of a group in Chicago whose outlook had much in common with the Catholic Worker philosophy. (This was not a good idea though there was plenty of good will all around. How it happened and how the mistake was recognized and what was learned is another long story which will not be told here.) Basically, being with the poor and living a fairly squalid lifestyle was part of this philosophy. For the two women, different as they were, the experience of the two years was one of a struggle to break free of this, in the end, deadening spirituality which yet has great emotional appeal since it feeds into the feelings of guilt which most people from a "comfortable" background have when they encounter the poor.

Living in Gary, Indiana, the two women were faced with a city threaded with corruption, in which most of the (mainly black) population is unemployed and without hope of employment, a place where the pollution caused by the remaining factories wraps the city in a permanent yellow fog, and where the pollution is prized as evidence that *some* industry is still working. They worked at distributing food, at helping people find furniture, and taking women and children to hospital. They were always on call, yet felt nothing was changing. Barbara taught a course which helped high school drop-outs gain their diplomas. Without text books, in a building with no heat in subzero weather, the students' enthusiasm and gratitude and hope were touching, and Barbara was a wonderful teacher.

But the temptation was to accept that responding to basic needs was enough. Can one keep on doing what is possible yet know that real change has to come another way? The patience of the dispossessed, their ways of coping and compensating, are admirable, yet to be patient is to play the game the owners' way. "Market forces" is another name of God. Unemployment is part of the system. In this God's religion, handouts are OK but to question the morality of the system is regarded as blasphemy. Let the unemployed move somewhere else, let them re-train! The fact that they have no money and that generations of oppression have made such people fatalistic or passive, is not considered. If they are unemployed, if they live in a toxic fog, that is because they are, at some level, not good enough. Their condition is God's will.

The experience, for both women, was painful and raised up deep personal issues. It did so also for a man in the program, Ted, who worked in Uptown, Chicago. He worked with a woman (the amazing Edwina Gateley, founder of the Volunteer Mission Movement — and *that*, as Kipling says, is another story) to open a house for prostitutes, a place of refuge, a place to talk, to get help, perhaps to begin something different. The experience led to a deep interior crisis and revolution. Work with prostitutes is an encounter with the most "homeless" of all women, the rejects, the despised, used and soon dead. Prostitution is society's final verdict on women. The apparent hopelessness of it all is demoralizing. Prostitution is economically profitable, a multi-million dollar industry which cannot be allowed to be seriously threatened, though the "rescue" of one woman here or there is not too important. Every now and then, it is true, mayors or police chiefs, goaded by public complaints, promise to "clean up the streets". For a few weeks police zealously tour the streets picking up rather more women than they usually do, and jailing or fining them. The women are more careful thereafter, for a while, to keep out of sight, but since no alternative is available they return to their pimps.

For a sensitive, intelligent man, trained to ask questions about social structure, called to believe in the possibility of transformation, the experience left no possibility of evasion. What does it mean to be a man in a society that allows such things to be done to women, and refuses to interfere or even to condemn? It condemns the women, of course, as societies have always condemned their scapegoats and punished them. It is the will of God.

Another mission trainee, Pat, went to work in a community for the poor in Atlanta, Georgia. Radicalized by her own experience, she could judge what she was seeing in this city that was grooming itself as a convention city, attracting the trades and the big corporations. To encourage this, the city has declared a "vagrant free" zone, and thc homeless who had slept or sat in the parks were removed. The dispossessed have no ownership in the city they live in, they have no homes, and so naturally no private bathrooms, and since there are no public toilets, and urinating in public places is a criminal offence, they spend a lot of time in jail, which is the only "space" where it is considered appropriate for them to be. Pat understood what was happening. The will of the god of commerce is a clean and beautiful city with well kept parks and luxury hotels. If the "others" — the ones who do the jobs nobody sees, and the ones who can't even do those — have no decent (or even indecent) place to live, well, that is how the system works. It is the will of the system.

In West Virginia, where Mary Kay worked for two years in a shelter for abused women, the will of these and other gods is spelt out more explicitly. The insecurity of jobs, the corrupt politics, the low wages and lack of safety precautions in the mines, the evidence at every turn of the contempt of the owners for the lives of those they own: lack of health care, no public transportation (plenty of trains for the coal) and poor education in dirty and ill-equipped schoolhouses. These things create the anger, depression and despair which breeds violence against women and children. It is how things are, it is the system, it is the will of God. Those who challenge it certainly will not gain public office, they (or their families) may be shot at, they will certainly be denounced by the preachers for questioning the will of God, whatever His name may be.

The dispossessed are so because that is how things are. It is God's will. Some of these men and women in the mission program originally chose to serve the poor out of the traditional theology that does not question how things are but calls Christians to relieve suffering. The actual experience, as well as the alternative theology they had helped each other to develop, made it possible to feel that this was adequate. They, too, experienced the rage of compassion, and struggled for a different theology, which shouted out that the will of God is the wholeness of all people, in the land which God gives them.

Yet the theology which attributes prosperity to God's favor and support may have originally been an expression of a sense that goodness, experienced in an abundance of crops and children, is not merely the result of human skill but of the human ability to be in touch with, and serve, the energetic source of life and growth far greater than itself. In our cultural experience this authentic sense of interdependence in creation, and with a creator (God somehow needing praise and celebration as well as *people* needing God's life-giving power) has given way to other forms of expectation of divine favor. It is understandable that people precariously defending their homes and livelihood against invaders should also thank God if they succeed in overcoming the enemy. It is a short step to assuming that victory is a sign of God's special favor, and defeat a sign of God's disfavor (or of God's incompetence). The reaction to this experience of rejection may be to express repentence and seek to propitiate the God or gods, much in the way women learn to repent and to propitiate the men they are perceived as having offended. Alternatively, the vanquished may decide to change their God in favor of a stronger one. The victors, on the other hand, secure in their efficient God, feel licensed to regard the vanquished as essentially inferior (since God does not like them) and frequently to enslave them. The enslaved then either accept this theology and their status under this God of the victors, or deny it and find another. Some black slaves imported into America learned to accept the white God and His "will" that they be slaves, but others continued or developed a secret theology of their own, with a different God who hated their oppressors and promised eventual freedom. But the will of God in the minds of the victors is that they dominate, and that the vanquished submit and accept their status also as God's will.

At this point the connection between will-of-god theology and ownership of land becomes clear. The victors are those who possess the land; the vanquished, the slaves, are those who do not possess land and therefore do not possess themselves, for, lacking land, they exist on it only at the will of their masters.

In societies where there is no slavery as such (now and in the past) those who do not own land are, just the same, lesser persons. They earn a wage, they pay rent, and are therefore at the mercy of those who pay the wages and receive the rent. They can lose income or home at any time if the owner so decides. In capitalist societies (which include so-called "communist" states as well as openly capitalist ones) the issue of land ownership as such is less publicly clear because transactions are expressed in terms of money rather than actual land; big corporations express their wealth in numbers of dollars rather than numbers of acres. Yet, ultimately, land is still the basic issue. The company owns the land on which the factory, or service industry, or mine is located, therefore it controls the employment there. Who works there, at what wage, for how long, and under what conditions is not decided by those who work there but by the owners. A corporation may also indirectly control land it does not legally own if it controls the market for products from land it does not own, (which may be whole counties or even nations). It can dictate what is produced, and how much is paid for it and so the income and life-style of the legal "owners". Corporations and cities also own the land on which apartment buildings stand, as well as the buildings. Who lives there, at what rent and for how long, and whether or not the building is well maintained, is not decided by the inhabitants but by the owners.

If the company owns the land, no one else does. In Appalachia the owners of the mines and oil fields, who therefore control the only sources of employment, also own eighty-five percent of the land. What is left is land at the bottom of steep valleys, always subject to flooding; most of the flooding is caused by strip mining, which means the removal of the trees and top soil so that afterwards rain does not soak into the soil but rushes down the bare mountain sides in destructive torrents of mud which wash away houses or whole towns. In this very fertile and beautiful country the inhabitants lack the land to feed themselves, and are therefore totally dependent on the owners of the land. The fundamentalist religion of the area teaches people to accept their poverty as the will of God and to seek salvation by commitment to Christ within that way of life. This theology is extraordinarily helpful to the owners.

This is the contemporary western version of the will-of-God theology, but it is world-wide too. The primitive theology of God's blessing on the victor and rejection of the vanquished, which is reflected in some of the psalms and histories of Hebrew scripture, takes on a new form of a considerably more destructive kind. The "victors", the beloved of God, are those who possess land, wealth, power. If they are religious they feel that this power is a sign of God's approval, and they get together at prayer breakfasts to give thanks for all this approval, which they feel they deserve. If they are not religious they still feel they have an indisputable right to what they have, they feel themselves somehow superior because they have it. When some individuals lose this wealth they begin to lose confidence, as if they had lost not only their wealth and power but their identity. They often become depressed; their God (acknowledged or not) has abandoned them. The "vanquished" in our terms are all those who (whether they were once owners or never were) depend on the "owners" for all the circumstances of their lives. This includes even the highly paid. Their "vanquished" status lies in the fact that they have no ownership in the land. They may be called citizens but if they lose their jobs they may sooner or later lose their homes (even "owned" homes) and so their right to respect. As they slide down the social scale they will be less favorably treated in court if they are accused of wrong-doing. They will be regarded as a problem and a burden, seen as inadequate and potentially criminal, so deep in our culture is the sense that God (some kind of patriotic deity anyway) approves of the prosperous and disapproves of the poor. But prosperity ultimately depends on ownership — and ownership is ownership of the land.

The earth has become property. Property is something with which you can do as you like, as long as you do not obviously harm someone else's property by your ownership, and the "someone else" is interpreted as someone with virtually equal wealth, since the "few possessions of the poor" are easily taken away if the rich see a need for them, and the law protects property — large property, that is, not the property of the poor.

The comfort, or even livelihood, of the poor is sacrificed to the need for more for the rich. In this enlightened era, for instance, the number of cheap lodging houses for single people of very low income has dwindled away to about one tenth of what it was even twenty years ago. The houses have either been converted to expensive apartments or condominiums, or torn down to make way for them.

All this is not exactly described as God's will, but (even among people who feel sorry for those rendered homeless) is felt to be inevitable, part of the will of some kind of power. The name of this god is, perhaps, "market economy" or "supply and demand" — the demand is for more homes for people with money, so the supply is created, at the expense of the poor. This god must be served.

The fact is that the vast majority of citizens accept as inevitable and right the notion that only some people possess the land rights and resources and do what they like with them.

When, recently, a movement began in Massachusetts to include a 'right to housing' clause in the State Constitution (on a par with the 'right to education') there was an outcry from people who felt that housing could not be a 'right.' Housing was something people had to qualify for by being in a position to earn an adequate salary. Statistically, 1% of

Americans own 25% of the nations' net worth and the wealthiest half of that owns most of the 25%. Also between 1980 and 1984 an income shift of $25 billion occurred from the bottom 80% to the top 20% of the population and this trend is continuing. Those who possess a great deal receive great respect. They give commencement addresses, their private lives are watched with avid interest, their opinions are asked about everything from foreign policy to 'teen pregnancies', for they are regarded as sources of wisdom. They are, in fact, those chosen and blessed by God, they feel it (even when they are atheists) and so does everyone else. When one of those blessed ones encounters disaster or disgrace the reaction is a curious mixture of glee and superstitious fear. The fall of the mighty satisfies everyone but it creates doubt — theological doubt. Perhaps God's blessings are not to be trusted after all. Perhaps the deity is tricky and malevolent rather than benign. But the moment of dread passes, we return to the adoration of the blessed rich who possess the earth.

This very peculiar state of mind is a matter of profound theological conviction. That is not how it is described but that is what it is. Western society has learned to live comfortably with gross inequality and all the suffering that goes with it because at some level of unquestioning faith it is known that this is the will of some kind of deity, and His will is known by the rewards He bestows and the punishment He metes out.

This kind of theology naturally results in a sense of energy and enthusiasm among those who see themselves at least within reach of the blessings of possession. One of the major social phenomena of the eighties was the "yuppies"; the young, upwardly mobile professionals, well trained, energetic, confident and highly paid, manifestly blessed by Him. They felt good. Conversely, this theology deprives of energy those who feel themselves rejected. They, too, accept their situation of powerlessness and insecurity as God's will at some level, and since this is so they must be inadequate. They subscribe to the same faith in rewards as proof of goodness, and know themselves as not good. And however hard they work they will still be not good. There are ways to dull that sense of worthlessness, or to compensate by exercising power over those still more inferior, but in the end the only way to comparative contentment is acceptance. This is how it is, this is the nature of life, this is His will.

This kind of theology has embedded itself so deeply as to be unquestioned, below the level of conscious choice or challenge. It sanctifies and glorifies the possessors, and justifies whatever means they use to maintain and increase their possessions.

And at the same time the specifically religious version comes in to provide compensation for those who are deprived of their homeland. It acknowledges that, no doubt, they are sinners, but there is a way out, they need not look to the more usual compensation of drugs, drink, sex and violence. There is a better way. To return to where I began, religion becomes an alternative emotional system which takes the rejected and (while not altering the results of this rejection) gives them meaning and even hope.

Don't change things, don't make choices, accept it all as God's will. Before looking at an alternative theology of the will of God, here is one final picture to add to those I began with. In a church in a public housing development outside Dublin the congregation for Sunday Mass consisted of very young families, the median age perhaps twelve, scarce a grey head to be seen. Some men, but mostly young women and children. The development is new, hundreds of houses (quite good ones) placed in a barren area deprived of trees, and also deprived of recreational facilities, public transportation or shops. (One small grocery store for the whole development.) There is 50% unemployment. There is, however, a church and a school, and the priests struggle, with commitment but without much conviction or imagination, to give some meaning and direction to the lives of people who clearly don't matter to the country they call their own. They are exiles in their own land, living in a kind of ghetto far from the places of people who matter. On this Sunday, as usual, the church was noisy with babies and small children, there was clapping and good loud singing of familiar hymns. But this Sunday was not quite like the others, for there was a visiting mission priest who had come with a group of lay people to bring a special message from God.

The priest stood at the lectern, and his voice dominated even the chatter of the children. It was the Sunday after Easter and the gospel story told how Thomas put his hand into the wounds of Christ and acknowledged him Lord and God. "You too can touch the wounds of Christ, you can know him as Lord, you can be *happy*," boomed the priest. He spoke with knowledge and feeling of the suffering of the poor — the unemployment, the wife-beating, the truant and rebellious teenagers, and for a moment it seemed, incredibly, that he could be about to show these people the way in which Jesus had, in fact, recognized such experiences, pointed to the cause of them and proclaimed a different way. But this man, with all the emotional power of a good voice and an excellent rhetoric, was proclaiming something very different. He was calling these people — mostly women — to find joy and peace in the acceptance of their suffering. "If your husband beats you, that is the gift of Jesus, so that you can be close to him," he told them. "If your children grieve you, pray for them, accept the suffering. You are without jobs, but reach out to Christ and he will heal you!" He went on and on. The message was clear. Don't challenge injustice, don't try to change — accept suffering, and find joy in it as God's will. And that evening there was to be a meeting in the church hall for those who wanted to "touch the side of Jesus". But there were some angry faces in that church.

How is it possible to break through a mentality that is reinforced at every level both religiously and socially? The need to do so is not a matter of merely "spiritual" concern. Until this mindset can be changed the whole superstructure of injustice which it supports remains basically unchallenged. Any help given to the victims of the system has to be merely peripheral to society's real concerns, and there will always be those who question the morality of even minimal aid for the poor since, as we saw earlier, in this theology the poor are poor by their own fault and must change themselves in order to receive the blessings which belong to the good.

This kind of theology therefore is the cause and the justification of the spiritual numbness which enables the comfortable to continue comfortable in the face of the suffering of others. If there is a theological cause, the way to break out of this numbness has to be theological also, and it has to do with women, and with land.

CHAPTER FIVE

"SUMMON THE MOURNING WOMEN"

Acceptance of God's will in the sense explored in the last chapter forbids anger and grief. If suffering is God's will, is redemptive of itself, then to express grief or anger at painful events is an act of rebellion against God. This is the message for poor women, whether in a religious or secular form. Women, who, as they explain their plight to the Welfare worker, show anger, are met with rebuke and hostility — they are questioning the system, and don't deserve help. Those who, remembering as they speak, break down and weep, provoke irritation and contempt. They are questioning the will of the God (whatever God rules the Welfare system) instead of accepting the punishment appropriate to the offense of being poor and rejected, and so being grateful for any assistance available.

Reflecting on passages from both Hebrew and Christian Scripture the Wellspring group found very different doctrines. Jesus, on his way to Calvary, was followed by women who dared to mourn for him — in their need to voice their lament, braving the presence of both hostile Jewish authorities and Roman military officials wary of public unrest. Jesus responded by telling them weep, but not merely for him: "Weep for yourselves and for your children." His whole life had taught him that the lot of women is to suffer most from any public disaster or oppression. He did not rebuke them, or tell them to look beyond suffering to glory, he simply redirected their grief.

All his life Jesus himself gave expression to his grief and his anger at what he saw being done to the poor, and specifically to women. The searing contempt for men who used a woman as scapegoat is apparent in the little story of the woman taken in adultery, and is an example of how he felt and acted. He stood in the tradition of the prophets who raged and grieved over the oppression and suffering of the poor and yet called to repentance and hope, and his last words to the women of Jerusalem acknowledge the need for prophetic grieving, as an essential aspect of redemption. Far from being a rebellion against God, anger and grief at oppression — including one's own — are essential for personal and social transformation. This chapter, therefore, pursues the theology of "God's will" to uncover the God who calls to grief and anger, the God who addresses women specifically and perceives the loss which is mourned as loss of the land.

It has become a commonplace of therapy that if a person is depressed, and feels "stuck" in life, it is often necessary to get in touch with suppressed anger and grief created by some hurtful past experience. This is often one which has not been allowed expression because to feel anger would involve recognizing that a parent or parent-figure has behaved in "bad" ways — an admission social and family pressure refuses to permit. Once the anger can be expressed there is a possibility of healing. We have seen this many times at Wellspring, as women who have been rejected and denied affection as children come to the point of recognizing this and being angry. Then, perhaps, they can begin to cease to feel that all their problems are their own fault, and cease to look for yet another abusive relationship to fit their sense of their own worthlessness. Anger is the emotion which reacts to what is perceived as evil and threatening, and it energizes to control and if possible to overcome the threatening thing, while grief is the encounter with, and the process of, the experience of loss. The two are linked, because anger is often the reaction to the evil which has caused loss. Grief is the way to liberation from the paralysis that can occur if people cannot move beyond anger — for anger is appropriately used to open up action, and sustained anger without appropriate action turns inward and destroys the angry one. This kind of anger implies the refusal to grieve, because to grieve is to admit that something is indeed lost, and cannot be recovered. Through grief it is possible to move on, to act, to create anew.

Until the grief comes — grief for a lost childhood, for a parent who is "dead" as source of comfort or love — the anger cannot liberate fully. Grief signals that something is gone, cannot be recaptured, it lets go of fantasies of the might-have-been, even fantasies of revenge, and it experiences reality as painful, but prepares to move on.

Anger and grief are tools of liberation, and they are part of the prophetic task, as I discussed in an earlier chapter. They are the way to break through the numbness imposed by the false God whose will sanctifies injustice. Anger and grief are theological statements. When Jesus raged and wept, and called others to do so, he was echoing the experience of Jeremiah, prophet of the fall of Jerusalem, who foresaw, tried to avoid, and then experienced, the destruction of his nation and all the horror and misery that went with it. Jeremiah expressed what he experienced as God's anger and grief, which human beings must enact if they are to be saved.

The prophet Jeremiah labored to get his countrymen to recognize that their way of life — their economic system and their politics — were leading them steadily to disaster. God was no longer going to lead them in battle or rescue them from their enemies because they were no longer behaving as God's people. The rich oppressed the poor and the priests looked after themselves at the expense of the people, getting rich in the name of God. Jeremiah saw ahead conquest and devastation and exile, and he saw no way to avoid them because there was no willingness to acknowledge wrong in a situation that benefited a number of people.

Those in power were doing exactly what they do now. "Each deceives the other, they do not speak the truth, they have accustomed their tongues to lying, they are corrupt, incapable of repentance." (9:4) They claim "wisdom", but wisdom is justified "by the lying pen of the scribes." (8:8) They oppress the "alien, widow and orphan" and say "Peace! Peace! But there is no peace," because those in power — kings, priests or prophets — are concerned for their own dishonest gain and are no longer capable of shame or repentance. (Calling a deadly weapon "the peace-keeper" is the kind of double-think which would not have surprised Jeremiah.)

Jeremiah saw hope, but only through acceptance of what was happening, not as *good*, but as a way of national "re-sensitizing". The people had been numb, they needed to come to life. They needed to *experience* the evil and not lie about it. Only so could the terrible experience become fruitful in hope. And we notice that Jeremiah was definitely not counseling passivity, or a rationalization that what was about to happen was God's will and therefore good. Jeremiah portrayed Yahweh as angry, he described the evils committed and the results to follow in terms of cause and effect which Yahweh would set in motion, out of a sense of bitter disappointment and anger. Jeremiah himself was angry at the crimes committed against his people by their rulers, and devastated with grief at the results, and he knew that this grief was essential if there was to be healing. Healing? One day, it is sure, but not yet — *now* is the time for grieving.

Grieving is not easy. Annie was a young woman of twenty-two who had had three pregnancies, two ending in abortion, and her little boy was in foster care because of the chaotic life-style which had endangered his life through neglect. Her own neglected and unloved childhood had left her emotionally immature and she went through a series of unsatisfactory relationships with men who cared little for her, always seeking the love she had never had. When she came to Wellspring she had been written off by the referring agency. She was pregnant again, and wanted this baby very much, but because of illness resulting from her insecure and unhealthy life-style she lost the baby. Meanwhile she was still hoping to regain custody of her first child, yet knowing she might well fail. This woman had lost her childhood, had effectively "lost" her parents, had felt obliged to "lose" the possibility of motherhood twice, had had little time with her surviving child, and finally had lost another longed-for baby. She had been neglected, despised and abused by the men she turned to. She had no home and no job and her health was causing concern. Yet it seemed impossible for her to grieve. She understood clearly what was wrong, why her life was chaotic and dependent, yet she struggled always to present an "I don't care" face. She denied the misery that consumed her, and only at moments could let a few tears come. She needed to grieve, for her dead babies, her lost childhood, to mourn for the wreck that had been made of her life. Instead, the bitterness turned inward in sickness and depression. She needed to grieve and could not, for grief is a skill hard to learn in a society that rushes to smother all signs of it lest anyone should suspect that all is not well. To Annie, also, we cry "Peace, Peace," when there is no peace.

For Annie, the beginning of healing did come, and it came through a memory that broke open her terrible numbness. One morning, coming into the kitchen to make breakfast, she began to weep, and could not stop. Nancy took her aside, and when she was quieter, asked her what had happend. The reply, comic and yet wonderful, was "raisin toast."

In her neglected and arid childhood there had been one person who cared for Annie. Her grandmother had sometimes rescued the child, often at two or three in the morning, from the barrooms where her mother had taken her. Then she would take Annie to her own home, comfort her, and fix her cocoa and raisin toast. But the memory of the love, and of the toast, had been buried by the years of bitterness, until that morning someone was in the kitchen making raisin toast. The special smell of it met the girl as she came in, and she remembered, and grieved, and then laughed, and then cried some more, and Nancy wept and laughed with her. And the healing began, and the transformation, and the long slow journey of hope. (Therapists know, that for a person who has been emotionally hurt and damaged, the possibility of healing may depend on whether or not there was one person who cared, and showed it.)

Jeremiah looked at his people and saw that like Annie they needed to grieve and could not. They were numb, proclaiming peace and prosperity on the brink of war and famine. So Jeremiah cried out to those who could teach this precious and life-saving skill. In an amazing passage he called on the women, because women are those whose traditional role includes the duty of mourning. In many cultures besides Jeremiah's there have been women who were hired as professional mourners, so important is their function perceived to be, and in most times and places the women of the neighborhood customarily come to help the women of the family to mourn to dead. So it was natural for Jeremiah to turn to the women at this time of need.

"Call the mourning women! Let them come!
Send for those who are best at it! Let them come!
Let them lose no time in raising a lament for us!"

Yet it is not enough for the women to grieve and mourn, the whole nation must mourn.

For this to happen the people must have teachers; the women must lead others —

"that our eyes may run with tears
and our eyelids be wet with weeping.
Yea, the wailing is heard from Zion:
What ruin is ours,
What utter shame!
For we must leave the land,
Abandon our homes!"

And this grieving process must continue in the time of exile. Through Jeremiah God gives to the women the task not only of being themselves mourners, and teachers of mourning in their time, but of passing on their skill so that the next generation may take up the work. The purification, the repentance through grieving, is a long process, before it is time to return.

"And you, women, now hear the word of Yahweh,
Let your ears take in the word God's own voice speaks:
Teach your daughters how to wail,
Let them teach one another what dirge to sing.'"

The women, and their daughters, and all those taught by them, are to grieve because only by grieving can new life come. And these women are to lead in mourning a death, but it is not the death of an individual, even a king or great leader, nor are they to mourn only the many deaths that are part of the disaster which is upon them, though there are indeed many of these:

"Death has climbed in at our windows,
and made its way into our palaces.
It has cut down the children in the street,
the youths in the square,

corpses lie like dung in the open field,
Like sheaves left by the reaper,
with no one to gather them."

The picture is starkly reminiscent of so many news pictures of ravaged countrysides; Cambodia, Afghanistan, Lebanon, El Salvador. But these deaths are happening because of something else. Jeremiah weeps, and needs help in mourning, for the loss of God in the land, and the physical and spiritual desolation which follows.

"Sorrow overtakes me, my heart fails me.
Listen, the cry of the daughters of my people
sounds throughout the land.
'Yahweh no longer in Zion?
Her ruler no longer in her?'"

If God is absent, there is a reason: it is the presence of false gods. In parentheses Jeremiah has God ask, "Why have they provoked me with their carved images, with these Nothings from foreign countries?" The "Nothings" are the same gods who comfort the people who cry "Peace!" when there is no peace, who claim God's blessing on their accumulation of wealth. They cling to illusion, as Jeremiah points out, and therefore are numb and deaf to the impending disaster. They are like the women who seek escape from their loss of themselves in sex and the illusion of love it gives for a time, in drink or drugs, in fantasies of prosperity or of a perfect mate, covering up the pain, refusing to grieve because that means admitting how much is truly lost and gone.

But the underlying disaster, and the death which is to be mourned, is the loss of the land, *because* God has departed from it — or seems to have departed because nobody is any longer able to perceive God. The people don't perceive God because they have replaced the liberating theology of Moses and the prophets with the enslaving theology of the idols of wealth and power who deprive people of real choices, enjoin submission as a religious duty, and discourage mourning as morbid and unhealthy and subversive. The disease is incurable because nobody is admitting there is anything wrong.

"Is there no balm in Gilead anymore?
Is there no doctor there?

Then why does it make no progress,
this cure of the daughters of my people?''

But the cure has to begin with the pain of knowing how bad the illness is:

''Who will turn my head into a fountain,
and my eyes into a spring for tears,
So that I may weep all day, all night,
for all the dead out of the daughters of my people.....
raise the wail and lamentation from the mountain,
the dirge for the desert pastures,
for they have been burnt: no one passes there,
the sound of flocks is heard no more.
Birds of the sky and animals,
all have fled, all are gone.
'I mean to make Jerusalem a heap of ruins,
a jackal's lair,
and the town of Judah
an uninhabited waste land!' ''

And what seem to be the words of a commentator underscore the message at this point: ''this is because they have forsaken my law which I put before them and have not listened to my voice and followed it, but rather their own stubborn hearts and foreign gods.'' The loss of God and the loss of the land, with all the deaths it involves, are inseparable.

It is actually just after this in the text that the summons to the women is placed. Jeremiah sees the women as the ones who can bring the only kind of healing that is possible in such a situation. They are to mourn for the loss of the land, for all the lives destroyed in the loss of the land, all of it because *God* has been exiled. And because God is exiled there is no spirit in the land, nothing to make it home for God's people.

It would be tempting to reflect on Jeremiah's picture of a land without vegetation, birds or animals, since as a race we are actually beginning to create such an emptiness by our exploitation of the earth's life systems. That is indeed something to which our prophets' grieving has to address itself, and women are taking a greater and greater part in that public grieving which can lead to awareness and repentance.

We shall return to that. The purpose of the last chapter was to look at the devastation threatened, and indeed already caused, by the theology of the will of God which turns out to be the religion of a monstrous idol, a "foreign god" who is nourished by lies and sustained by apathy and the denial of death. In this chapter, we looked at Jeremiah's alternative theology of the will of a God who is angry at injustice, grieves for the suffering of the week, and calls on the people to begin the long, painful process of healing by learning how to grieve. The will of God is the life of the people in the land, but it can only be recovered by repentance.

Jesus had the same idea, and spoke of it and lived it. God is the life-giving Abba who sends rain on all, who is concerned to provide for everyone, who discourages discrimination — how do you know if another is good or bad? God forgives and welcomes, and the welcome, as Jesus lived it, simply means ignoring all the categories which divide people and subject one group to another. His disciples asked him why a man was blind, was it his sin or his parents? Jesus replied that that was irrelevant, what mattered was that God should be glorified in the man's healing. When two of them wanted to call down divine punishment on the Samaritan village that refused the group hospitality, Jesus rejected such a notion of God's will. That isn't how God operates. Let's go somewhere else.

Jesus spoke to, healed and made friends with women, and other neglectable people, because his God did not love people because they were wealthy, or even particularly good, but because they were willing to be loved. He had a difficult time disabusing his followers of the idea that rewards of power and prestige would naturally follow discipleship, thus signifying that they were approved by God. Discipleship was likely to lead to quite other consequences. He did not foretell, and eventually embrace, suffering and death because they were "God's will" in the sense of being somehow good things, but because the road to Calvary was the only road open to him if he were to be faithful to the vision he was called to proclaim. It was therefore the only way to life.

Jesus, too, found himself up against a false theology of the will of God, one used to keep the poor poor, and to allow the resources of the land to be exploited for the enrichment of the rich, both by ownership and by religious taxes. Jesus, like Jeremiah, saw that the reign of the "foreign gods" who disguised themselves as Yahweh had led to an apathy and denial in both rich and poor. Like Jeremiah he experienced anger and grief and called on others to share them. He took a hard look at the reasons why the people were sick and harassed and poor. His social analysis was accurate and penetrating, and he expressed it in terms of both political and spiritual realities. He described the people as harassed and dejected, "like sheep without a shepherd", in words recalling Ezekial's great denunciation of the fake shepherds who clothe and feed themselves from the flocks, but allow the sheep to be wounded and lost. Because of this he was "moved with compassion" for them, a word meaning the kind of gut-churning rage which people feel when they confront gross misery and the arrogant selfishness which allows and profits from it and calls that God's will. But as well as describing the situation of the oppressed in terms of traditional biblical symbols he also pointed out very directly the methods and motives of the oppressors. "You tithe mint and anise and cumin", taking every little bit of possible tax revenue from the hard-won earnings of the poor, even down to their herb patches. "You bind heavy burdens on people's backs and don't lift a finger to help carry them." The rich wore "purple and fine linens": — the purple dye was an import, a sign that the wealthy Jew was adopting the life-style of the wealthy Roman, while their own kin sat at their gates in rags and hunger. Jesus recognized then, as we must now, the religious hypocrisy that has become so entrenched in its own self-justification that it is impervious to compassion, teaching that those who suffer are justly punished and, above all, that God wills the political and economic status quo.

In the end, when Jesus wept over Jerusalem, the beloved city, he was confronting disaster for the city that could have been prevented if his words had been heard, but they were not heard and he knew it was too late. Minds and hearts were closed. The way forward was through the seasons of pain and death.

Before that death it was a woman who "anointed him for burial" because she understood his grief and his purpose and could break through the mindless optimism which his male disciples were still trying to maintain. And on the way to Calvary, as we have seen, it was the women who wept for him, and whom he bade to weep "not for me but for yourselves and for your children", for the task of mourning is longer than you think. The women were less likely to be deaf to his words, not because they were necessarily "better" but simply because they were the essentially dispossessed. Unless they identified totally with their men (many did and do) they had not the same stake in the preservation of the status quo, in which they had no choices and no control. So they heard more easily and responded more deeply and with less rationalization. For women, the idea that God willed openness, and ignored barriers, was a whole new world and a welcoming, rather than a frightening, one. Some of these women around Jesus had begun to make choices, to dream, and when the dream seemed to be dying they knew that, at the least, it was worth mourning. It was also worth caring for, when dead, and this is why it was women to whom the life beyond the mourning (but only through mourning) was first revealed. "Blessed are those who mourn, for they shall be comforted."

The will of the God of Jesus is accomplished in the making of difficult and often painful choices. The God of Jesus wills the healing and life that come through truth, and that therefore requires the uncovering, not the covering up, or evil. The favor of this God is known in the exchange of life and love, in the breaking down of barriers and the growth of awareness and wisdom between people, and between all creatures, in the mourning of what has been good but is lost. This God's will is discerned in the times when oppressed and wounded people such as those women, and the women at Wellspring, begin to recognize their own worth and to reject the verdict of worthlessness which has kept them bound and without energy.

The recovery of a sense of God's will is inevitably the recovery of the sense of the land, which of course is why the false theology is so important to those who hold the power in the land and deprive others of their homeland. Jeremiah promised that eventually people would come back to a land restored and purified, and second Isaiah (the prophet of the return from exile) sang a song of the new land in which there is no oppression but all live in peace from the fertile earth. That, said the prophet, is God's dream too. It was also Jesus' dream, for the "little ones" whom he would lead to the pastures rightfully theirs, in which the hungry would be fed and the dirge of mourning in exile become the song of return.

In the last chapter I tried to bring to the surface and describe the way a false theology of the will of God underlies destructive attitudes in individuals and in the whole culture. It is, in effect, a system of idolatry since it means obeying the demands of "foreign gods" whose "foreignness" is demonstrated by the fact that obeying them negates human development personally and socially. It is "foreign" to humanness.

In doing this I discoverd in the agonized insight of Jeremiah how the role of the mourning women is at the heart of any possible healing, and how that same reality was true in the experience of Jesus. And the mourning is for the death of hope in the land, it is the mourning of those condemned to exile.

First then, why is it the women to whom the task of mourning is assigned? Certainly, not only women have the capacity to grieve. But, as the employment of professional mourners in some societies indicates, grieving is not regarded by any society as a purely private affair to be indulged in at will by a person who experiences loss. Society decides when grief is appropriate and permissible, and who is to express it. It is considered permissible for little children to grieve when they lose a toy, babies may cry when they "lose" a person who goes out of the room. (It takes time to become sure that the one who is not visible is not "dead'). On the whole, children are permitted to express grief openly for a dead puppy, a "treat" cancelled, a beloved auntie who has visited and then gone home, even a death. However, the tendency very soon is to try to cut short the grief, to distract them, to replace the lost toy or pet, to assure them that auntie will return, or that grandma is "in heaven" and is watching over them, or simply to cut short the grief: 'That's enough, now." From older children, and even sometimes from little ones, expressions of grief are too difficult for the adults to deal with, and so they are not allowed. Children are often not taken to funerals because it would "upset" them, which really means their open grief would upset the adults.

But girls are allowed to cry more than boys and their grief is less upsetting. At a very early age boys are told "you're too old to cry," and if they cry they are reproached and even punished. This restriction is not a peculiarity of our society, it is virtually universal. In some cultures men are permitted to cry and do cry and are even admired for their grief in moments of high emotion such as a death or a patriotic occasion, but their display of grief is expected to be comparatively brief, a necessary concession to feeling but not something that can be allowed to shape consciousness or decisions. In all cultures, even those in which men take part in mourning rituals, it is felt that the women not only may, but should, be more deeply involved in the mourning process.

One reason for this is that it is perceived as necessary in a patriarchal society for men to make decisions and be in control of the whole situation, which means land and property and the people who service them. For "lesser" men the control of property may be very limited, but in order to feel themselves men it is all the more necessary to them that they feel themselves in control of what they do possess. But to be and remain in control of things in any degree means to impose loss on others. The "others" exist only to preserve and serve the possessions of those in control, and therefore those "others" must inevitably suffer loss of choices, loss of possessions or the opportunity to acquire them, loss of liberty (to learn, to move, to change) and even loss of life.

The poor often perceive such loss as natural and inevitable. That the possessors dispossess is in the natural order of things. When Wellspring bought its third house, a semi-derelict lodging house, we decided to re-hab it to become a reasonably comfortable home for single men and women who can never afford apartments. This was done with the help of rent subsidies, so that the tenants pay very little. While re-hab was going on it was necessary to relocate the existing tenants, and they were assured they would come back. They took some persuading. One man, leaving the house where he had lived among filth and cockroaches for many years, paid his rent, and said, "I'll be moving on, you won't want the likes of me here when it's all clean and new." Nancy, (who had got to know the men during the year in which she managed the house before funds were available for re-hab to begin), explained yet again that he *was* wanted, that he could come back. He would not believe it. "The men in town are saying, 'Don't believe them, nobody does up a place like that for nothing. They'll get you back and then double the rent on you.'" It took a while to convince him that the whole purpose of the re-hab was to provide him, and others like him, with a decent home at a rent they could afford. That is not how the possessors are expected to behave. Compassion for the losses of the poor are simply not good business, for to be liable to grieve over the suffering involved in loss of homes or livelihood would make it impossible to continue in possession. If the master is to remain master he must severely restrict the occasions on which it is appropriate for him to feel grief.

One of the most horrible results of the many patriarchal systems is that so often those who are dominated identify with the master (who is, it seems, blessed by God). Women of a privileged class, themselves denied freedom of purpose, join in the oppression of the underclass, as white women still do in South Africa. Prisoners join with guards to oppress other prisoners. In all such cases those who oppress (even when they themselves are oppressed) must not allow themselves to feel grief at the suffering they impose or witness. If they do they are betraying the masters, who have decreed that this suffering is necessary and right.

It has happened at times that among the homeless women at Wellspring there has been one who is, perhaps, less intelligent or more worried and confused than the others in the house at the time. There is often a tendency for the others to render her outcast in subtle ways, more especially if she happens to have come into the house a little later than the rest, among whom bonding has already happened. With little silences or giggles, or by making plans that pointedly exclude her, sometimes by pointing her out to the staff as a source of problems, they exclude her and condemn her. The compassion they feel for each other's pain, and which is often a source of great strength as they try to confront their problems, is denied to this one. They will not grieve with her or for her, and (at least behind her back) may even laugh at experiences of hers which in another would evoke sympathy. This is a reflection of their knowledge of how a patriarchal society works. They have learned that it is appropriate and necessary that some should be rejected, and their own experience of rejection, the unexpressed anger they feel, is vented on the one who can give them the sense of power and control of which they have been deprived.

Fortunately, it is usually not hard to change this dynamic. Most of the women can be helped to realize what they are doing and to change it. Sometimes this is done at a house-meeting, which happens weekly and which everyone in the house attends. These meetings are times to assign chores and decide times to do one's laundry, but they are also times to try to surface underlying tension and conflict in the house. Most of the guests are quite unused to attempts to resolve conflict by talking — their experience is that conflict is dealt with by one side silencing the other, either by loud argument, or by violence, or sometimes just by ignoring it until it becomes part of the furniture of life. So it is not easy for them to hear or respond when such issues are raised as the tendency to exclude or scapegoat one person. To have the victim publicly express how that feels is to open up a whole new perspective. There is a wealth of compassion in the human heart, trapped and disallowed but waiting to be released, and the situation can change radically after even one such encounter. The change is awkwardly done, with embarrassment, even reluctance; there are rather obviously contrived gestures of friendship, small gifts, even letters, (because saying it in a letter is easier than saying it out loud).

More often such situations at Wellspring are confronted in one-to-one meetings between the guests who are involved and their "primary worker", which means whoever on the staff is assigned to them as informal counselor, guide and advocate during their stay in the hosue. The "primary worker" and her assigned guest meet at least once a week, generally more often, and work on all kinds of issues from budgeting to divorce. Often a good deal of trust is built up, and in time sensitive personal issues can surface. And over and over again at the heart of the complex emotional and practical problems culminating in homelessness is the sense of loss, and the lack of ability to grieve for it. Like the child forbidden to grieve over a toy that, to her, was a friend and companion, these women have learned that their loss is inevitable, or their own fault, so grief would be stupid. That is why they easily slip into denial of the reality of another's loss. But it is also why, once trust is established, a time may come when grieving begins.

The woman reclaims her right to feel compassion, for others and for herself. She learns that it is not "self pity" to mourn an abused childhood or rejected love or lost dreams, but rather a right compassion for that child, that lover, that dreamer, who is one's self.

This leads to awareness of a second reason why mourning becomes the task of women. This is that once women accept permission to mourn their own losses they easily become capable of the compassion which issues in mourning for others — known individuals, and the unknown millions of people who suffer, or the vulnerable earth herself. Once true mourning begins, and numbness is broken, domination and exploitation of others becomes harder, and easier to recognize and change when old habits recur.

Compassion makes it impossible to abuse and dominate, at least as long as it lasts, though it can be lost or forbidden as we have seen. Also the absence of the need to dominate allows compassion. This is at the root of the role of women as mourners. Domination renders the dominated non-persons in the feelings of the master, because that is how compassion is avoided. Compassion is for people.

Compassion is subversive if it creeps in among the masters. This is why the compassion of Jesus — his feeling for the way the poor had been deprived of their birthright — was so threatening to the power structure which depended on that deprivation that in the end it was necessary to get rid of him. The compassion of Jesus was subversive and dangerous precisely because he was a man — and a man who could exercise authority, engage in debate and do all the things that men are supposed to do. The trouble was, he did not only use his authority on behalf of the dispossessed: this was and is permissible as long as it doesn't actually alter the pattern of dominance. Public philanthropy has always been regarded as appropriate for the powerful. But Jesus publicly mourned for the dispossessed, and with them, appropriating to himself the role of the victim. It is socially acceptable and undisturbing for women to mourn. "Men must work and women must weep", as an old song says. Since women are without power their tears do not upset the pattern. On the contrary, they perform an important social function. By this permissible grieving they make sure that an exploitative society has feelings. (It is possibly not coincidental that the Victorian era, when the exploitation of the underclass for the enrichment of the upperclass reached levels undreamed of before, the rituals of mourning also became more elaborate, lengthy and expensive than ever before; but they did not indicate any great compassion for the deaths of thousands in the mines and factories, the profits from which paid for the plumes and black satins of wealthy funerals.)

But now, women are engaging in a kind of public mourning of the kind Jeremiah envisaged, and it is an expression not only of private grief but of precisely that rage of compassion which Jesus experienced, and Jeremiah and other prophets before him, and since. These women are doing the same kind of passionate social analysis which has always fueled the prophet's rage, but it is women who are doing it, and the effects are significantly different.

Women are grieving publicly in Western society for the destruction of the earth and its people which is going on and which may result in the death of earth. Like the woman who broke an alabaster phial of perfume over the feet of Jesus, they are mourning a death that is still in process. The reaction is not unlike that of the guests at the house of Simon the Leper. "Why waste all that time and energy and money protesting nuclear power, or protecting whales or rain-forests? These people should go home and spend it — spending keeps the system going — and give a little to charity because that's only right."

When women get together with other women or with men, to plan and carry out actions against the deployment of the weapons which may destroy all life, they are engaging in just such a duty of public mourning as that to which Jeremiah called the women of his time. But in doing this, now, they are stepping outside the bounds assigned to mourning. They are not doing the usual women's job of mourning the private dead (even dead presidents and popes and kings and rockstars). They are entering the arena of politics. Political mourning is not usual or acceptable. Politics is expected to be about power, and now women, and men also, have introduced compassion into politics and this is extremely dangerous.

If one needs to be convinced of just how dangerous this political grieving is felt to be it is only necessary to read accounts, or see newscasts, of the behavior of British police and American military towards the women who maintained the women-only peace camp at Greenham Common, outside the heavily armed perimeter of the base where nuclear weapons were stored. None of these women had ever been armed, they had done nothing more dangerous than sing, weave colored wool through the barbed wire, and periodically shake the fence until it fell, as a kind of symbol of the vulnerability and folly of patriarchal structures. But mostly they were simply there, camping and cooking and talking and trying to keep dry, or warm, (or cool). Yet they were beaten, sometimes severely, insulted, their tents and equipment taken away and destroyed, even the plastic shelters they took to instead of tents periodically removed. They were imprisoned in high security prisons as if they were dangerous criminals.

Men also have committed themselves to this kind of political mourning. What is happening is that many men are permitting themselves, as people also now threatened with anihilation, to experience the deep rage of compassion which is a human capacity long denied them. Domination no longer makes any sense if what you dominate is being destroyed. The need to save what is threatened with death at last breaks down the cultural conditioning to dominance.

But it is the women who lead because women, by nature and culture, are the preservers and the healers. The mother of a child experiences acutely the fear of loss because the child is so fragile. Women experience the extreme fragility of all life, and until they are educated out of it they are in touch with the cycles of the earth which also gives birth, and nurtures and heals and loses, and brings to life again. Women were the first agriculturists and in many places still do the farming. (In Kenya the word for marriage is literally "to acquire a hoe"). During the Ethiopian famine we saw photographs of women obliged to watch their children die because the land had died. In America, women see children sicken and die when water sources are polluted, and they mourn, but also, since they are not wasted by hunger, they are able to rise up in rage and act. The links between the health of the earth and the health of the people is becoming very clear. So, now, men and women perceive that being a mother, and also being a father, means the nurturing not only of children, or even of people, but of the whole earth because the earth is one organism. It is sick and in danger of death. The destruction that has happened and is threatened must be publicly mourned so that all can see and understand, and the energy of compassionate rage may seek life beyond this death.

These mourning and raging women know that, if there is a way to healing, it will not come through the good will of the possessors of the land. The possessors will fight to the end, even if it is their own end, to preserve their dominance. They may yield something to public opinion, or to fear of electoral or commercial loss if protests or boycotts are effective, but they will yield as little as they can, and take it back if they can. That is why the healing of the earth must also be a new "housekeeping" enterprise.

The earth is home: we have no other. The earth's women are coming to realize that their own age-old dispossession is likely to become the homelessness of all creation, if the earth becomes uninhabitable.

In the collection of essays called "Reclaim the Earth", Anita Anard tells a story of women in a remote village in Northern India called Resi, who did something very peculiar — they hugged trees. What they were doing was saving the future of their families and their land. Hugging the trees, women and children prevented seventy lumberjacks from felling the oak trees as the contractor had sent them to do. The felling was part of a profitable enterprise — trees were felled to make equipment for export. Laborers were being imported, and new power lines and roads were built, and soon schools and clinics went up — but only the well-paid incoming workers and officials could afford them. The trees were big business, and this brought "prosperity" to the region.

The local people had lived off the forest, which supplied their basic needs and provided a surplus to sell. The new ways offered jobs, but tied them into an economy that depended on export. Moreover, as the trees were felled, the fragile topsoil was washed away, resulting in major floods which washed away bridges and roads and farms and people. This was serious enough to make the government pause — and to decide to replant trees, but only quick-growing pines which were a profitable cash crop. But pine needles do not absorb rain as fallen oak leaves do, and the people could not live from such forests. The men were compelled to leave home to work for the incomers in order to survive, so all the work fell on the women, who were left to sustain the home economy as best they might. Still the loggers came, to destroy what was left of their livelihood.

So in 1974 the women organized. Their anger took action. They and their children went out and wrapped their arms around the trees, crying out, "The forest is our mother's home, we will defend it with all our might."

This movement, called "Chipko Andolan" (meaning "hugging movement") forced the State government to investigate the concern of the women. Its committee reported that 12,000 kilometers of sensitive watershed area was endangered by the felling, and the felling was stopped.

For all the creatures of the earth there is no other home to go to if this one is destroyed. Novels may speculate about the colonization of other planets when earth dies, but that is at best a remote possibility for a very few, and is more realistically an aspect of the massive denial of the threatened death which is entailed when the earth is a commodity to be bought and sold.

The task of breaking that denial, of awareness, and thence of grieving, and thence of repentance and homecoming (to whatever home is left) is a global one, and the task is laid on the women to teach the skills of anger and grief to all the people, so that perhaps all may repent, and come home while there is still a home to come to.

CHAPTER SIX
COMING HOME

What does it mean for the exiles to come home? The story itself, from which the perennially and universally powerful symbol is derived, gives us a way to understand what Wellspring is about, and how this little entity has meaning in the whole amazing phenomenon of home-coming. For the home-coming is happening — for women, and in, through and beyond them for all those efforts and projects and dreams and insights which are right-brain and feminine and different, and for all those, men and women, who struggle to live by them.

We survive in a world which lives still under the shadow of nuclear war and of "conventional" war, which only seems less horrendous because it can be less final. Even though the threat of nuclear destruction is lessened, the people who played war games still do so, and prepare to play the same kinds of games with different counters. The old and new money and power games continue to use the people and the environment. They create wholly unnecessary shortages leading to millions of deaths, and slowly and steadily poison the earth from which we derive sustenance — food, water, air. Some of the damage is already irreversible: the "greenhouse effect", warming the earth's atmosphere, creating deserts and melting the polar ice caps, may be slowed by stringent regulations of carbon dioxide and CFC emissions, but it is happening anyway. The underground aquifers which supply water for the millions in the U.S.A. are not only becoming depleted, bringing anxiety about our ability to provide water to meet all the needs (not to mention the pseudo-needs), but are also increasingly contaminated by industrial toxins, and by pesticide and fertilizer residues from farms. An aquifer is not like a river which cleans itself quickly once pollution ceases.

It will take decades, perhaps centuries, for aquifers to renew themselves, always supposing the water that seeps into them is not further polluted. We don't yet know what damage will be done when the nuclear waste dumped in the oceans is finally released from its casings, though scientists are pessimistic. Thousands of species of animals and plants have already been destroyed, and are being destroyed daily, and nobody knows for sure what effect this will have on the gene-pool of future evolution. In many places, the numbers of varieties of fruits, vegetables and grain, and breeds of animals, have been deliberately reduced, and hundreds prohibited from commercial use, for administrative convenience in marketing. The danger of this, if diseases become resistant to pesticides, is obvious. Fortunately, dedicated growers and breeders continue privately and sometimes illegally to preserve species which will one day be needed to save the food of the future. I could go on and on. Such facts become almost without impact, because we have heard them so often and also because they make us feel so helpless.

It is the sense of helplessness before huge powers which have no accountability that deprives people of energy and hope. Such must have been the feeling of many of the Jews in exile. Their lives were not necessarily unpleasant, in fact many settled down and did very well, adopting the systems and values of the culture in which they found themselves. But, for those who tried to keep in touch with their identity as God's people, the normal struggles of daily life were complicated by the personal and communal struggle not to be absorbed by the surrounding values (which seemed to work very well if prosperity were what one wanted) and to keep alive a hope which was more than sentimental nostalgia for the good old days. Among them, prophets never ceased to remind them of the past and call them to the future.

Before the disaster of the Babylonian invasion, and the subsequent exile of all the "professional", skilled and educated people, as well as the royal and priestly classes, the accepted philosophy had been that the purpose of God was to preserve a privileged place and situation for the chosen ones, protecting them from enemies and ensuring prosperity for the righteous. In the process of building up a wealthy nation the memories of the great Exodus experience, the Covenant of fidelity between God and the people, and the sense of responsibility for each person within the community of Israel, had been eroded, but the highly centralized priestly bureaucracy, alongside the royal one, claimed a mandate from God and stood as sole interpreter of God's will. That *God* would let them down was unthinkable. Troublemakers like Jeremiah — denouncing false leaders, calling for submission to the invader, and prophesying doom — were clearly unpatriotic, subversive and dangerous and should be silenced.

It all sounds very familiar. Western culture, proclaiming principles of liberty, equality, democracy and impartial justice, created systems of government, commerce and religion which effectively maintained a permanent underclass to provide cheap labor, justifying this as "the nature of things" and the will of God. How much liberty and equality you could have depended on your economic usefulness. Democracy stopped a long way short of creating a system that responded to the needs and wishes of the common people, as opposed to those of business interests, and impartial justice was not and is not normally the experience of the poor, racial minorities, or women. When some people have raised their voices to point out these truths and to further point out that the churches, in the main, have at best condoned and at worst actively supported this state of affairs, they have been denounced as unpatriotic ("un-American"), subversive, athiests, dupes of Communism, disloyal to country and church. They have been deprived of media exposure, they have lost their jobs, been imprisoned. If they had been able to exchange reminiscenses with Jeremiah they would have discovered much in common.

But silencing prophets is not an effective way to deal with the issues raised by them. The people in power could put Jeremiah in a cistern but Jerusalem was sacked anyway, and those who had refused to heed the warnings were taken into exile, along with the thousands of "non-political" people who thought they could avoid doom by keeping quiet and leaving the decisions to the experts. Quietly, without acts of Parliament or of Congress, without headlines or announcements, the basis of Western society has been changed. Its direction, its government, its conditions (political and environmental) have been taken over by huge military and business interests, which are in practice accountable to no one but themselves. They rule the Western world, and also the "Third World" which has provided such wonderful replacements for the sweated labor and child-labor fortunately outlawed (though still surviving) in Western countries. "The women in those countries are so skilled with their hands, they don't expect much and don't mind monotonous work." "Their land is inexpensive." "In those places we don't have to deal with unions." These are recent and typical quotes from smug and happy representatives of corporations building factories in "undeveloped" countries. In this context, "prosperity" means wealth for foreign business and for a minority of local owners and bosses. It means, for the ordinary people, loss of traditional livelihood subsistence wages, long hours in atrocious conditions and no unemployment or sickness benefits.

Thus the people are in exile; homeless, confused, dependent on the controlling will of the owners they never see. Many deal with this by identifying with their rulers, as did many of the Jews in exile. This can lead to prosperity and power, without explicitly renouncing the worship of the god of the Exodus, thus changing the divine image to fit the foreign gods who bring security and wealth in the new land. So now we have the "Moral Majority" (whatever it calls itself now), having as their God the rewarder of the rich, the confiner of women, the hater of "leftists", who calls for nuclear vengeance on the ungodly, meaning anyone who threatens white male dominance and the material interests of the dominant class or who questions denial of support to the poor, since the poor are sinners.

There remain the faithful ones, the ones who, in exile, struggle to recover a sense of who they are and what this is all about. Then, and now, they re-read the old stories in the light of painful disillusion. They discuss, pray, re-write, to discover the meaning that can show them a way forward.

They deepen their sense of identity as a people and, led by great prophetic voices, begin to express a sense of what it means to be God's people, but in very different ways. No longer the darlings of a God who exists to assure them perpetual prosperity and dominance, they identify themselves once more with those forebearers who came out of Egypt and discovered themselves a free people, responsible to God and each other for each person, every beast and field and olive tree. They discover through those folk memories and their present experiences what it means to be oppressed, and what liberation must be like: not the reversal of dominance, with themselves as the oppressors, but to become a sign of freedom to the oppressed. They are to be creators of a new city in which all have enough, in which no child fails to grow to maturity, and in which there are no such things as aliens, for Israel is only set apart insofar as it has a unique mission to spread the news that justice, peace and security are the intended inheritance of all people, not the privilege of a few.

This is exactly what has been happening in our world, as more and more people learn to recognize themselves as exiled from what is in fact their home: the earth — bountiful, beautiful but enslaved and persecuted Mother Gaia. Christians and Jews, and people of little or no explicit faith, have come together, in small gatherings, driven to re-assess the meaning of faith. They came disillusioned and angry at the failure of official religion ever to be aware of what has happened, let alone to respond to it except by bland cover-ups or a retreat into a strong denial provided by individualized, dualistic religion which either ignores oppression or somehow glorifies it.

People have gathered, sometimes, to address a particular wrong; to protest nuclear and chemical weapons, or homeless families, or pollution of land or water, or destruction of old neighborhoods and landmarks. Or they have come together out of the inner need to make sense of their lives and their beliefs. Like the exiled Jews before them, led by prophetic voices, they have explored, argued, studied, worked, hoped. They have discovered new meaning in old teachings, and realized that the meanings are not new, but were always there, but over-painted and altered by the hand of greed, timidity and fear. In Eastern Europe, at this moment of writing, the patience and hope of 'exiles', the voices of their persecuted prophets, have prevailed. In one nation after another the people rose up and threw off unjust and oppressive government. It is too soon to tell what will replace them, whether they will fulfill a new-old vision for humankind or, as the Jews did, repeat all the mistakes and sins of their predecessors in power. But they have demonstrated that newness is possible, that God can lead people home, if they want to come.

The "communidades de base", the "base Christian communities" of Central and South America, have become a world-wide message of hope. In countries where the Church drew its leadership from the wealthy and land owning classes, the gospel was good news for the rich, and for the poor virtual enslavement and dispossession, a call to submit patiently with the hope of heaven to comfort them. Then, suddenly, there were priests staying with the people, and in the fields and in the cities was heard a different message: God does not will oppression, God is Moses' God of liberation, Jesus came to call the poor, to proclaim the reign of God, to announce to the humble that they shall inherit the earth. In other places — in Haiti, poorest of all, in Aftica, in what the French called the "quart monde" of industrial oppression at the heart of "first world" economies, in black and Hispanic neighborhoods in America — the same thing was happening: the poor were reclaiming the gospel and committing themselves to the work of liberation. Led, at first, by priests and ministers, the communities were and are gatherings of friends; lay leaders arose, called together other communities and led them. In many, in time, male dominance was re-asserted and women relegated to secondary status, but in some, and those the most energetic and fervent, the women were and are fully equal, leaders also. In Nicaragua, women struggled to share the work of revolution, knowing the danger. The call was more important than family, than safety, than life. In 1979 a young mother in prison wrote a letter to her little daughter, and her words echo the vision of the prophet, the vision of Jesus himself, even though the language is not religious.

"This is a very important time," she wrote, "for people everywhere; today in Nicaragua, and later in other countries in Latin America and throughout the world. The Revolution demands all each of us has to give, and our own consciousness demands that as individuals we act in an exemplary way, to be as useful as possible to this process.

"I hope that someday, not too far off, you may be able to live in a free society where you can grow and develop as human beings should, where people are brothers and sisters, not enemies. I'd like to be able to walk with you, holding hands, walk through the streets and see everyone smiling, the laughter of children, the parks and rivers. And we, ourselves, smile with joy as we see our people grow like a happy child and watch them become new human beings, conscious of their responsibility toward people everywhere.

"You must learn the value of the paradise of peace and freedom you are going to be able to enjoy. I say this because the best of our brave people have given their precious blood and they've given it willingly, with great love for their people, for freedom and for peace, for the generations to come and for children like you. They've given their lives so children won't have to live under this repression, humiliation and misery so many men, women and children have suffered in our beautiful Nicaragua.

"I'm telling you all this in case I'm not able to tell you personally and no one else tells you these things. A mother isn't just someone who gives birth and cares for her child; a mother feels the pain of all children, the pain of all peoples as if they had been born from her womb. My greatest desire is that one day you will become a true woman with a great love of humanity. And that you'll know how to defend justice, always defend it against whatever and whomever would trample it.

"Well, my plump one, if I have the privilege of being able to see you again — which is also a possibility — we'll have long talks about life and the Revolution. We'll work hard carrying out the tasks we're given. We'll play the guitar and sing and play together. And through all this, we'll come to know each other better and learn from one another.

"Come, show me your pretty face
Lovely like flowers and freedom
And give me energy to struggle
Uniting your laughter and our reality
Daily I think of you
Imagining always how you are
Always love our people, and humanity

With all the love of your mother, Idania.
Until our victory, forever.
Free Homeland, or Death."

The child never did see her mother again. A month later Idania was killed by the National Guard. In Nicaragua the fragile achievement of a revolution made by young and often unwise but courageous and generous idealists maintains a beleaguered hope in the face of a mixture of military threat, economic blockade, and well financed subversion (a mixture typical of the tactics of power faced with the audacity of the poor to demand ownership in their own land). In other countries, men and women gather to share the gospel, to pray, to celebrate, working for freedom at the risk and often the cost of their lives, and knowing that they themselves may never come home to freedom. They ponder the message of Jesus, and the symbols of freedom and of return home.

As the old teachings become clearer, the new vision becomes stronger: the vision of home. It begins to seem that the return is actually possible. The little groups begin to try to create, among themselves, new ways, new systems — ways of being and doing, models of a different kind of society, harking back to the one Moses created out of a band of demoralized ex-slaves; not a "perfect" society but one based on the deep awareness of the interdependence of all people with each other and with the land.

It takes more than the experiments of scattered and politically powerless exiles to change the dream of return into an actuality. For the Jews, the opportunity came when the Babylonian Empire fell before the Persian Cyrus in the late fifth century B.C.E. Cyrus was an enlightened ruler who knew what few autocratic rulers throughout history have known: that oppressed, landless people are apathetic, difficult to control, unproductive, and a constant source of possible unrest. He believed in giving people control over their own lives and land. The prophet of the return, the "second" Isaiah, hailed Cyrus as Messiah, God's anointed, and he was indeed the liberator. It was he who decreed that those of the exiled Jews who wished might return to their own land, taking with them all the treasures looted by the Babylonians from the Temple. They were to rebuild Jerusalem and restore the half-abandoned and neglected countryside to prosperity.

There is, however, something more to this than the unilateral decree of an enlightened despot. If the Jewish exiles had allowed themselves to become, as a whole, thoroughly assimilated into the culture of Babylon, would Cyrus have sent them home? He gave them a choice, knowing some would choose to stay, but aware that there was a substantial body of educated, informed, and energetic Jewish people able and waiting to undertake the huge task of restoration. Cyrus's decree made possible the return but Cyrus's decree would have been empty words without the prior existence of a recognizable body of people able to carry it out. The long years of grieving, repentance, study, hope and organization brought about the possibility of return. Cyrus provided the opportunity.

There is no world Emperor of the late twentieth century to decree the return of the exiles. Yet, strangely enough, something similar is happening in our time. Steadily, the pressure on the wielders of power has built up, even though they have denied its influence at every step: the protests and demonstrations (from the action of a few doing civil disobedience to the march of a million through New York); the peace camps; the impact of environmental studies; famine and famine relief efforts; the increased public anger and anxiety over issues of pollution; the aftermath of the Vietnam war; loud voices of women's organization; the civil rights movement and its follow-up; movements of liberation in Third World countries and in Eastern Europe and China; mounting anger at huge defense budgets. All these things and more have had their effect. Politicians listen to public opinion, to an extent, and governments (even dictatorial ones) know the limits beyond which they cannot hoodwink and mislead the people or totally silence discontent. But also, not all in power are deaf and blind to the things that have touched and changed the attitudes of ordinary people. People in power for a long time were not actually admitting that there was a change; however what seemed to be happening was a kind of tacit permission to try alternatives.

In many countries they tried them, with effect far stronger than anyone expected by local Cyruses. Open denunciation of the system in the 'free' world is still only allowed as long as it can be disregarded as merely an exercise in free speech by a bunch of weirdos and leftists who read "Mother Jones" and probably don't eat enough steak. Cyrus is firmly in his seat and nobody who is "anybody" is suggesting a palace revolution. But something *is* happening. People are being encouraged to move into obvious gaps in the "system". This is often touted as a return to traditional values of "self-reliance" and a move away from top-heavy government. "The system" is still untouched, or thinks it is. The "gaps" in the United States are very large: the enormous loss of housing, the prevalence of wages too low to support a home, farming families bankrupted by a distorted agricultural market, unhealthy food produced by agri-business, patches of near-total unemployment in old industrial areas, soaring medical costs and women without pre-natal care, a rising infant mortality especially among black people, and elderly forced to pauperize themselves before they can get medical care. And so on and so on and so on.

These things constitute, for us, Jerusalem in ruins. We have been given permission to return and do something with that mess, we have even been grandly presented with access to sources of technical expertise, and some limited funds (which came out of our taxes anyway). The permission to return and rebuild is not exactly generous — our opportunity lies in the areas with which the system is not able or willing to deal. Meanwhile it goes on its way, creating more "gaps". However, while being realistic about the motives for this "permission", we can also realize that it is a real opportunity in two ways. First, it allows us to try to put in place and operate in small ways those alternative models of living that we dreamed of or experimented with in the time of the exile; but also, if we can do this successfully, it gives us a public platform from which to educate and inform and to step up the pressure on the holders of power. That they are not impervious, we have seen. What we have now is some little space in which we can claim "this land is home to me", and move on in the hope that one day all the world can be home.

The Wellspring project is a little part of the return home, at the same time that it is a part of the experience of exile. The reality behind this paradox is that it is necessary to come to the point of recognizing oneself as exiled before it becomes possible to embrace the opportunity of going home. That is difficult. Part of us is invested in Babylon, it isn't a bad place, it provides us with cultural and material benefits. Also, learning to acknowledge that one is an alien and trying to keep in touch with that as the price of integrity and hope is a very uncomfortable business. So we veer between the two states. Wellspring is a place where some women who have been enslaved begin to learn to claim freedom, but then, — like the people of Israel — adopt the normal cultural definition of freedom which is the power to be acceptable to society and accumulate possessions. Some of them may then make the further, painful journey into consciousness of exile, which those of us in the Wellspring community have made along with so many other women and men of our time. Only when we know clearly that we are exiles can we begin the return in truth and integrity.

This is very important, because the opportunity for a true return, to reclaim the land for God's people and build the human city, is also the opportunity for colonization by the empires of the likes of Reverend Moon, and Pat Robertson, or any of those who blame the victims and look for "cures" for poverty and sickness by preaching what Bonhoeffer called "cheap grace" and denying that anything is wrong with the system that crocodile tears and handouts won't fix. With virtually unlimited funds, and a tempting offer of total spiritual security here and hereafter, such people can do a lot with some of the gaps where "the system" does not operate. And generally speaking "the system" likes them better, because they do not challenge its operations but endorse them. But this is not the true rebuilding of Jerusalem, this is the erection of a slave colony. This is why it matters so much that we allow ourselves to experience the sense of exile, and keep in touch with the meaning of that symbol in our relationship with the culture in which we live and of which we are a part.

Quite a good example of how this works in practice is the way food is used at Wellspring. When the first members discussed what their common life would be like, before they moved in, there were various points of view. Mine, coming out of a background of whole-food and organic gardening, emphasized those values both from a nutritional and from an environmental point of view. I wanted these values to be part of the Wellspring philosophy. Others, less convinced but interested, emphasized the obvious need for economy — we were going to have to manage on a very slender budget, and this small budget was a direct result of our decision to commit ourselves to "alternative" work and lifestyle, unsupported by the large salaries that some of us, at least, could command if we chose. Nancy's contribution was the sense that a careful food budget combined with care in the preparation of food was a statement about our attitude toward the use of resources, combining appreciation of good things, avoidance of waste and excess and a spirit of celebration. This particular input sharpened later, as we began to feel, and say, that it was important to us, sheltering women in poverty and on Welfare, to provide food that women in poverty could afford, and which could still be nourishing and appetizing. In this kind of discussion and development, there was a clear sense of identifying ourselves as exiles — that is, consciously affirming values and customs which were unlike those of the surrounding culture. But as people already in some degree beginning the task of restoration, we chose behavior which was in accord with the vision of the land as home for God and God's people. There were different ways of interpreting this but the aim was clear.

When we moved in, and had to make decisions about what to buy, some conflicts arose. We joined the local food Co-op, to support this initiative, to be part of something that was "people-based", and not profit-based. It helped to reduce some food costs, and gave us access to organically grown food. But the Co-op did not stock only organically produced food, and the organic vegetables were more expensive. Which was more important, our budget or healthier food? This has never been settled among us in principle, though in later years the whole issue of farming practices, how food is treated, and how those who grow and process it are treated, has become a clearer issue for us and affects our buying decisions. For instance, we supported the Nestle boycott, and also the boycott of grapes and other things produced by workers who were not allowed to unionize, were underpaid and worked without protective clothing on crops sprayed with toxic materials. We had a formidable list of products we couldn't buy because of the conditions of production or the low wages of workers. Some items on the list produced moans of protest, when they included some favorite food! Here, the tension between the inevitable aculturation and the desire to create something different becomes quite painful!

People who are going through the trauma of homelessness, not to mention what might have gone on before that, are not in a state of mind to deal with unusual or "different" food, and for that matter those serving the homeless are not all whole-food freaks like me, and long for the fleshpots of Egypt! Many guests who come to Wellspring have subsisted on junk food, eating anything that seemed quick, easy and comforting, too harassed or depressed to care. Many have no experience of "family cooking", and cannot envisage themselves as cooks at all. At the same time they need nourishing and restoring food to help them regain health and hope. We tried to develop a balance, providing food that was attractive, reasonably familiar, comforting but also nourishing and healthy. Some guests will pick, refusing almost everything as a kind of protest, others soon become accustomed and enthusiastic, want to learn how, and say openly that for the first time meals became interesting and worth taking trouble over. We make whole-wheat bread, but also serve the softer, store-bought brown bread, but seldom white, unless it is donated, or is Italian garlic bread to serve with spaghetti! We use comparatively little meat, and guests find they enjoy dishes with cheese, or cheaper cuts of meat used in smaller amounts. Instead of being a problem, less meat becomes an opportunity and a pleasure. Thus we consciously try to embody the values of "home" in the experience of exile.

Then there is the garden. In the first year a friend loaned a rototiller and cultivated an area of what had been grass. We sprinkled lime and a load of manure, fenced the area and planted vegetables in four-foot square raised beds. (The water-logged nature of the ground in spring and fall makes raised beds essential.) The harvest that first year was modest, but constant additions of compost, and as much peat moss and manure as we could afford, transformed the heavy clay soil (the only flat land on the property is alluvial clay of the old river bed) to friable, fertile loam. We mulched with grass cuttings and hay to keep down weeds, but resorted to black plastic when hay was too expensive. The compost bucket in the kitchen is a source of comment — occasionally critical — but people get used to it! In the summer and fall the garden helps to keep food bills down, providing food grown without chemical pesticides or fertilizers and there is some bounty left over — strawberries for jam and to freeze, tomatoes to can and freeze, pears from two trees in a good year, potatoes and other roots to store. But the garden takes a lot of work from early spring to late fall, and we have sometimes wondered whether it was worthwhile since we are unlikely ever to be able to grow enough to provide all our vegetables. To do that, feeding a household of up to twenty people, would be a full time job for at least one energetic person. So why do we do it?

Again, I think the root of it lies in our attempt to create, in little, the sense of wholeness, or literal "rootedness" in the land, which our vision tries to capture. The cycle of the seasons, waiting for crops to ripen, one kind succeeding another, is very different from the taken-for-granted abundance of the supermarket vegetable and fruit shelves. These are filled with produce grown in chemically fertilized soil lacking essential minerals (and draining off to pollute rivers and aquifers), sprayed and treated with toxic chemicals both before and after harvest, grown, picked and packed by workers who are underpaid, and work in atrocious conditions exposed to chemicals of known toxicity. This produce is shipped hundreds and thousands of miles to make sure we have everything all year round whether it is locally "in season" or not. Most people have lost any sense of what "seasonal" could mean, except perhaps for the corn season in New England, and pumpkins which mean Hallow'een rather than food. So we have abundance at low cost, but at high profit to the grower. We know this, yet we are part of this system, and year-round variety and abundance is expected. Either we use it or pay higher prices for organically grown produce. The tension is real. The values of the place of exile war with the vision of home, so we work hard to make our small quixotic statement of faith in a different possibility.

Wellspring is a house of celebration. This has many meanings, and food is only part of those special days of festivity. Some guests return for Thanksgiving (ours is celebrated on the Sunday before, to allow this). We celebrate birthdays, and the days when families are ready to move to their new homes. Christmas, Easter, holidays, special days to invite old and new friends to share the house, a dinner before a Board meeting — all these occasions keep the vision alive, all in their own way celebrating recovery of the land. They include music and singing — Mark comes back with his guitar and his beautiful baritone, or brings his Morris dancing friends to dance on the lawn. Or there is bobbing for apples and pumpkins and candles for Hallowe'en. But food is part of all celebrations, because food as a way of affirming shared life is as old as the human race. Special food, lovingly prepared: and the preparation is part of the celebration, as everyone is drawn into chop, peel, mix, set out extra tables and chairs in the chapel when the dining room is too small, arrange flowers, sweep, dust, put on best clothes.

On the Sunday before Easter (because that is the day people can come) we celebrate Passover. We use a modified form of the traditional Seder ritual. It is not a Christianized form, but it is shorter and simpler than the full Passover Haggadah, for people with no previous experience of the great ritual. Forty or fifty people sit down to dinner, with the ritual beside each plate, and the ritual foods — bitter herbs, salt, water, unleavened bread (made at home), wine, charoset.

A "mother" and "father" are chosen to lead the ritual, candles are lighted, and children ask the ancient questions and are answered by their parents or another adult. "Why is this night different from all other nights?" "We were slaves unto Pharoah in Egypt and the Holy One brought us out with a strong hand and with outstretched arm." Prayer and responses pass from mouth to mouth. People who never go near a church or say a prayer become absorbed in this extraordinary rite, sharing the ritual foods, at first shyly, then with more confidence, reading the responses, singing the songs. Then "dinner is served!" and people experience the mixture of worship, food and friendship of which there is so little in most formal religion. Yet it is at the heart of Judeo-Christian faith, and opens up a sense of what the Christian Eucharist has to be about. "Blessed be God for the land and for food!" everyone cries at one point. The exiles asked in Babylon, "How can we sing the songs of the Holy One in a strange land?" But for a short time we *are* at home. "And now our feet are standing within your gates, O Jerusalem!"

After dinner there will be the fourth ritual of thanks, later there will be more singing, and later still all those dishes to wash, all those chairs and tables to put away. But the sense of hope and confidence that carries everyone cheerfully through the long day is more than a passing euphoria.

This is a very special time for us, for this age-old feast of the Jewish people in which we are privileged to share is the celebration of the past, the present and the future. It celebrates this present time, the thanksgiving for sufficiency of food and the land from which it grows; it looks back to the great liberation from oppression in an alien land, bringing God's people back to their own land, where they might grow this food in peace and freedom; it looks forward to a time when this land may truly be home to those still dispossessed and landless: "Next year in Jerusalem rebuilt".

When the exiles returned to their home, to a city long ruined and overgrown and a devastated countryside, discouragement was understandable. After all the dreams and plans, the reality was mud, shortages and quarrels. The Persian treasury had provided funds for rebuilding but it was hard to recapture the dream which had seemed so clear when they studied, reflected and prayed over the old testimonies of God's actions and the law-making and histories of the great days. One dilemma in particular seems very familiar to religious people now, as they struggle to find ways to rebuild the holy city of justice and peace. This dilemma stems from the very strength and integrity of those who, in exile, preserve hope and vision and do not allow themselves to be absorbed by the values of the surrounding culture, even though they must live in and from it. The Jews in Babylon, and people of faith in these last years, have found all kinds of ways to keep alive the essential sense of a distinct identity, not as a superior elite but as a people aware of a mission for the sake of all. This distinct identity is essential, without it they would never attempt the arduous journey home and the even more arduous task of rebuilding, yet it is a danger. If it leads to exclusiveness, suspicion of others' motives or customs, it will destroy the whole purpose of the rebuilding and merely establish one more intolerant cult, trying to impose its ideas on others. This fate has threatened to overtake some of the best and bravest of the prophets of return, simply because they meet with so much intolerance and misunderstanding that in self-defense they guard themselves with a mystique of difference — different language, food, clothes, life-style, — that keep others at a distance. Yet — how can they not be different? And isn't that the whole point?

Probably there is no perfect way to deal with this dilemma. Wellspring has seemed to some peculiar and suspect because it isn't natural for people to live together in one household (unless they are nuns or hippies). To others, Wellspring's unreligious flavor has been a scandal. ("Don't you read the Bible with the women? Surely nothing you do for them is any use unless they accept Jesus!") We cause scandal to committed whole-food and ecologically pure people, we also irritate those who find health "freaks" an eccentric nuisance. Wellspring is intentionally ecumenical and we interpret that broadly. Liturgies are celebrated there by Catholic, Episcopal, Methodist, or Lutheran clerics of either sex, or by a member of the community or a friend who may or may not be ordained. Most of its members are rooted in the Catholic tradition but its religious thought and practice draws from many sources, and its favorite prayer book is a Jewish one, written in inclusive language by members of a congregation in New England. And the music used at liturgy is as likely to be a modern folk or protest song as from a religious source, and typically we turn to Paul Winter's "Missa Gaia" with its celebration of the earth and its use of the songs of whales and wolves together with choir, organ and vibrant black vocalist.

This mixture — some might say confusion — came about over time, as we tried to find ways to express who and what we are, and stand for, in lifestyle and in worship. It was not planned, yet bit by bit it took shape, as individually and collectively, we sought for a way to realize ourselves and our guests as exiles and yet to model and celebrate a time and space for return and rebuilding.

I think perhaps the prophet of the return (the "third Isaiah") who wrote to encourage the despondent Jews camped outside their ruined city, would have understood why we do what we do. He, or she, was very much aware both of the need for clear identity and the danger of exclusiveness. The prophet had celebrated Cyrus as God's messenger, divinely appointed and inspired, but then called on rather chauvinist compatriots to look honestly at the sources of the hope for the future. Frankly he told them, we have to face the fact that those hopes come from abroad, from the lands where you have been aliens. You need to leave behind the land of your exile but you can't do without the nurturing ideas, skills, money, support which will ensure your future if anything can:

> "Lift up your eyes and look around,
> all are assembling and coming towards you,
> your sons from far away,

and your daughters being tenderly carried.
At sight of this you will grow radiant,
your heart throbbing and full,.....
.....for see, the ships are assembling,
vessels of Tarshish in the front,
to bring your sons from far away,
their silver and gold with them.....
.....foreigners will rebuild your walls
and their kings shall be your servants."
.....you will be suckled on the milk of nations,
suckled on the riches of kings." (Isaiah 60:4-5, 9, 10, 16)

To put it at its simplest and crudest, isolation and exclusiveness will not get you what you need to rebuild. You must learn to draw on the wealth of those you thought you could leave behind — and you should feel good about it, "your heart throbbing and full."

There is greatness and richness, not only of money but of art, thought and skill, in the land of exile, and it is needed for the rebuilding. To isolate ourselves is to doom the mission which gives us our integrity. We need not surrender to alien values, but learn to perceive the power and wisdom of God at work in the alien scene. We begin to guess, nervously at first but with increasing assurance, that the glory of God revealed in the return of the exiles shines also in places where we hadn't expected — or wanted — to find it. So we have the exceedingly difficult task, frought with almost certain mistakes, of discerning the elements in an apparently alien culture which, in fact, belong to the true character of the land which is home.

Wellspring has gone through its process of evaluation and planning. For eight years the group of people, itself undergoing major and difficult experiences of change and growth, had been trying to respond to the surrounding need. The need was limitless, the resources limited. To avoid disillusion, guilt, and frustration it became important to focus, to come together and decide what should be our direction. What are we really here for? Who are we? Resident community, staff, Board, volunteers, friends — the categories in overlapping circles of responsibility — what is the meaning of us? We look at past and present, interior strengths and weaknesses, exterior threats and opportunities, we dream, set goals. What is the nature of this enterprise?

The time during which this book has been written has not seen any pause in the unfolding of the story itself. In fact it was in the experience of a whole year in which I was trying to capture the story and the meaning of it that the development of the thing itself changed the form of the book. What had been intended simply as the story of Wellspring, and some reflection on that, acquired a theme and a focus — the theme of land, and the *essential* homelessness of women whose lives have been symbolically in slavery, but with very real suffering, or in exile, throughout most of human history.

It was only with time that it was possible to express *why* it was so important to have a garden, *why* festivals mattered, *why* indeed the provision of shelter mattered so much, and why eventually it was essential to provide housing as well, not just because people need homes but because the providing of homes for marginalized people is a manifesto, a proclamation of a different truth: it is not merely kind, or necessary, or even just — it is essential for the truth and health of creation that the exiles come home. The theological meaning of women's homelessness was not an insight that emerged immediately, it took time, it took years, it took a year of conscious reflection on the nature and purpose of the group, the development of a mission statement, of goals and objectives and strategies, and all the labor of committees and consultants.

Who are these people who reflect on their common enterprise even as it continues to unfold?

They are people whose common ground is a home.

The Board of Directors meets there, in the living room whose huge hearth proclaims that it was once the kitchen, dining room and general gathering place of the house. The Board consists of people who, in one way or another, find in Wellspring a kind of hope they don't find elsewhere — people of many skills and many points of view, and including, now, two women who were once, with their children, homeless guests of Wellspring. On the Board also are two volunteers, representing the many more who offer skill, time and enthusiasm to the work of the home, some every week, some occasionally. Their lives add another dimension, bringing a sense of varied experience; most of them are women, often from comfortable homes, with good education and interesting jobs, lives full of opportunity — yet they come not only to contribute their gifts but to know themselves as part of this making of a home, and homes. It is not "charity", it is the earthing of a vision.

As we reflected, the sense of ourselves as symbolized in the image of exile and return helped to clarify the sense of who we are and where we are going. This great adventure of return is one in which millions of men and women are engaged. If we relied on the reports of events as they reach us through the news networks, we might conclude that the exiles are powerless, engaging in futile day-dreaming that renders them useless in the real world. Yet, as I have suggested, the deeper evidence indicates an extraordinary power of renewal and hope effectively at work, all originating in such small and inconspicuous gatherings as that from which Wellspring has grown. Wellspring is an enterprise in which women and men of all kinds are involved, and which is itself part of a world-wide network of centers of work and hope and vision. Yet, the theme of the book is a theme of women, their homelessness, their exile, their return.

If this is a book about women, is that because I have a special interest in the plight of women, as a woman myself and because I work with and for women almost entirely? I don't think so. The enterprise of the return is the enterprise of a whole people, ultimately it must engage everyone, and yet there is an important sense in which it is, and must be, an enterprise of women. That may seem an odd claim to make when I am using as a central symbol a historical experience in which women certainly had a part but which was initiated and carried through chiefly by men.

There is a twist to that very story which helps to explain the claim that the enterprise of return is a women's mission. The sad fact is that the returned Jews did indeed rebuild city and Temple, but they did so on the old model of dominance and exclusiveness. The leaders of the returned Judeans rejected the help of others of the people who had remained behind in the land, and made permanent enemies of them. (The enmity between Samaritans and Jews and the contempt of Judeans for Galileans stems from that time.) They did not, as the prophet had urged, understand or welcome the contribution of other nations, except the financial ones. In their efforts to preserve the integrity of the nation they created a centralized, rigid, hierarchically stratified religious society. The shared enthusiasm of the adventure gave way to familiar class structures.

Not long after the return, Nehemiah, architect and leader of the rebuilding, cried out in anguish at the oppression he saw. Jews were exploiting the needs of other Jews, lending them money on their fields and homes so that they could buy corn in time of shortage to pay their taxes to the king. Some had to sell their children into slavery as pledges for their debts. "Our bodily needs are the same as other people's, our children are as good as theirs," they complained, "yet here we are, forcing our sons and daughters into servitude, and there is nothing we can do because our fields and vineyards belong to others." This cry is echoed even today all over the world, as parents see their children forced to work at low wages or to live on Welfare, because "our fields and vineyards belong to others" though for most poor people that connection is not clear as it was to the Jews. Nehemiah moved in and remedied the wrong at the time, but it didn't take long to reappear. The poor became poorer, the rich richer, and God was used to keep things like that. The Temple ritual grew in splendor and beauty, and kept the priests in privileged comfort — until yet another conqueror destroyed the beautiful thing once more and put out the lights of worship. Even then God's people did not learn. Roman rule restored peace if not sovereignty and the Temple was rebuilt, as the old pattern of dominance and exploitation continued, protected by a foreign rule which found them useful — they kept the people quiet and docile.

This has been the pattern of many revolutions which

began in joy and comradeship and ended in yet another version of oppression, so much so that many people feel that this progression is inevitable. The failure of the returning Jews is usual, yet it is surely not inevitable. The person who most strongly believed that it was not inevitable was the Jew, Yeshua-ben-Yosef, Jesus from Nazareth.

Jesus was convinced that the vision of the great prophets was not just poetry. He denounced the oppressive religious system that kept the poor helpless and guilty and the rich not only secure but self-righteous. He knew it could be different, and he began to put in place on a small scale an alternative model of religious behavior based on awareness of the inclusive love of God, the nurturing, forgiving, embracing God whom he called Abba.

This new way of being together certainly had leadership — his own, and that of those he appointed — but this leadership was accountable to the least in the group, it was the leadership of a mother who protects, feeds, educates and challenges the children and finally liberates them into adulthood to "go and do likewise!"

The most radical thing that Jesus did, in the rigidly patriarchal system of his time, was to include women among his friends and followers and to give them leadership roles also. It is not necessary, here, to present the evidence of this — so many scholars have done this, and more are doing so, and a recent book of mine *(The Re-Creation of Eve)* explored the meaning of this reality for women now. It is a central reality of the gospel event, and its significance is far deeper than the obvious fact that Jesus who came to set the captives free and heal the broken hearted would certainly set free those most completely enslaved, and heal the hearts most wounded — those of the women. Perhaps somewhere in his thinking and visioning, there was a very early memory of his homelessness, the insecurity, the dependence, and of the mother who coped with it all and gave him a strong sense of identity and hope, then and later. The revolutionary woman celebrated in the "Magnificat" may not have been easy to live with but she probably planted some seeds of awareness which blossomed later.

Some writers have named Jesus as a feminist, others have pointed out that the evidence is too scanty and ambiguous to support such a title. My own feeling is that it would be a mistake to describe Jesus as a feminist. He did denounce the treatment of women, and accepted women as equals, friends and fellow workers, whose special gifts he needed and valued, but in this matter as in other controversial areas he seems to have broken categories and flouted accepted behavior not exactly deliberately, but because the categories and divisions and exclusions were so meaningless to him that he didn't even bother to confront them. He just walked through as if they were not there, as indeed for him they were not. But integral to this profound and direct approach to people, men or women, and to his deep friendship for individual women and his compassion for many, was his experience of God.

Beyond the compassion and anger and grief that drove Jesus to liberate women there lay the image of God from which he drew that grief and compassion. The God of Jesus is a mother-god first of all, and the vision proclaimed by Jesus in the name of God drew on those images of Isaiah which present liberation primarily as a recovery of home: a place of caring and security, of abundance and health, of joy and celebration. It is a feminine vision, and Jesus' attempt to put in place the beginnings of its fulfilment depended a great deal on women — the women who opened their homes to him and to his strange collection of friends of both sexes. These women created the setting in which it became possible to envisage the relationships of cooperation and mutuality in which none need be poor or oppressed. Liberated by his extraordinary insight which put them in touch with their own divine power and mission, these women helped and enabled him to pursue his dream. And when persecution, and the disillusion and desertion of many, forced him to an anguished rediscovery of himself and his mission, the women did not lose touch with the essential vision, but walked with him the bitter road to martyrdom. It was the women who, when all seemed lost, were able to grasp the fact that the new thing had in fact just begun.

All this did not happen because these women naturally had a greater capacity for holiness, courage or vision, but because, as women, they were more easily in touch with the strange kind of God Jesus proclaimed. They knew about caring for people and letting them grow, they knew about the need to share and not dominate, they knew about making a home. They were the ones who gave birth and attended birth. They were the ones who grew the healing herbs, tended the sick, bewailed the dead.

They were not the only ones who knew these things, but they were the ones through whom this kind of knowledge passed, and they were less likely to lose touch with this wisdom, distracted by doctrines of power, control and competition.

At Wellspring, Holy Week is a special time to get in touch with the sense of what we are doing. The confrontation with the reality of failure and death, and the assertion of the hope of new life, are moments of challenge, self-searching. We create, from different sources, rituals that draw on ancient and traditional symbols, capturing a prayer of the third century, a reading from Guatemala, a chant from Taize. This is a language we are developing, that speaks for us and to us, yet is universal. Or is it? On these days, as to our weekly liturgy, the guests very seldom come. Jesus spoke to women and they understood. We, it seems, cannot speak that word in the context where it should be clearest, the place where we affirm ourselves as God's homecoming people.

Yet somehow, it happens, and we know that the new language is the true prophetic voice, however poorly we speak it. Like the women to whom Jesus spoke, homeless women in our house can and do recognize something that touches them. One year, we gathered to celebrate the Easter vigil. It had been explained to the guests, earlier in the week, but it all seemed very odd and irrelevant to them, something the staff wanted to do for reasons best known to them.

The lights all over the house were turned off, leaving one room for those who didn't want to attend. We were preparing to go outside and light a new fire in an old iron cauldron. Suddenly the separation seemed unbearable. Nancy went to the women and asked them to join us — please come—at least try—. So they came, nervous, giggling a little, polite but not too pleased. The fire was lighted, and blessed, the candle lit, the chant arose, the light spread, carrying candles through the dark house, lighting every candle we could find, coming at last to the dark chapel. The big white candle stood among flowers, the chant of the "Exultet", (ancient and strange and yet just right) blessed the rising of light out of darkness. It was Marygrace who sang it, coming back with her husband to share with us the time of rebirth.

The women listened, looked at each other, a little apart, wondering. There were the readings, commenting, telling, celebrating, bringing into our time the proclamation of victory over death. And the blessing of the water. It shimmered in a big dish before the table on which the candle burned. Water of cleansing, of birthing. Two by two, we came forward and blessed each other with the newly blessed water; one of the community touched a guest seated beside her, beckoned her forward. They touched each other with the water. Then two guests came together, then another community member and two more guests, in a laughing trio. One girl, big eyed, sat and watched but did not move. Nancy came to her, her hands still wet, touched her with the water and kissed her; the girl's face broke into a smile. Suddenly, we were not two groups, but one. The great symbols worked. It all came together. The room was filled with a sense of power and conviction; you couldn't pin it down, it doesn't last, in a sense, and yet it is real, it happened, it is remembered.

The women at Wellspring responded to the message without clearly knowing what it was. They are not unlike those who first heard it. Of course, it doesn't become a reality just by persuading a few to share a ritual. The ritual comes alive because the new life is being nurtured and supported day by day, and above all because there is "something there" which already knows it. It is a feminine "something" to do with the power of birthing and the experience of suffering and rejection. It is a "something" for both men and women but it is difficult for a masculine society to hear because such a society is obsessed with the need to maintain its control.

Basically, the vision of the prophets and of Jesus was a "right-brain", feminine understanding of human life. This is why the church which tried to carry on his work so soon lost touch with his vision, in a world where the feminine was despised. This is why the whole of later Western culture, built on ideals of total control of nature and of lesser human beings, has driven into exile those insights and skills which Jesus perceived as central to the establishment of the reign of God, and which the women around him grasped — if not fully, at least deeply.

The reign of God that Jesus proclaimed is not vague or impractical. It is an earthy and earthly job of making the planet a place where human beings can be at home with each other and with God. Jesus spent a great deal of his time and energy defending his vision against people who couldn't or wouldn't understand it — most of his parables were addressed to his critics and opponents — and in the end it was only in his death that the thing he lived in and for could enter deeply enough into the consciousness of humanity to become invulnerable to death. Because of his willingness to let go his earlier hopes and yet never to let go the reality which was his whole being, he carried with him into the very heart of the human mystery the elusive yet enduring knowledge that God's sons and daughters can actually live as such in the home which is God's earth.

That knowledge has kept on popping up throughout history, inspiring thousands of efforts to create a different kind of life even in the midst of oppression and incomprehension and apathy. Whether it was the monastic communities of Hildegarde or Hilda, or the Beguines in Flanders, or the Diggers in seventeenth century England or the Amish in Pennsylvania or Ghandi in India or Danilo Dolci in Italy, or the women of Greenham Common — flawed and fantastic though they may be, the exiles struggle to find a way home.

The earth is our Home and we have no other. Now, it seems that there is finally sufficient awareness perhaps to save it, and nurse it back to health, though the scars will remain forever. This is women's work, feminine work to be done by men and women who have that combination of gut-level insight, compassion and anger with clear, honest observation and thought, by which the ruined land may become once more home for the dispossessed.

Women discover that they are exiles, and then begins the journey home. It is difficult to overcome generations of conditioning that abdicate responsibility, that expect others to control what should be everyone's home. It is difficult to let go habits of accommodation, the training that tells us our job for which we will be rewarded is to be a productive part of the alien system, and to help others to feel comfortable in it.

It has been difficult to the point of despair to continue the work of Wellspring year after year, as new members came, became discouraged, or did not understand the vision, and left. It has been hard to make sense of working long hours to achieve what seems to be so small an effect.

It is very small — or is it? Even in the last year, more than forty homeless families found homes, began to remake their lives; many keep in touch, come back for a monthly "Wednesday Night Supper Club," organized by Mary Kay, to renew friendship, talk about issues that matter to them or watch a video on some topic they choose. There is a newsletter for former guests, they write some of it themselves, follow each other's progress, help each other out. There is the beginning, in this, as understanding grows, of a strong network for change. It all centers on the home, their common ground. It is, literally, the place where they began to reclaim the earth as their home, because they knew themselves, just a little, as people who matter.

In the last year, five men and five women found homes in the single rooms of the lodging house, sharing a kitchen, beginning to enjoy cooking, developing small friendships. They are people who have been hurt and despised and pushed around, but in beginning to enjoy a home and share it they are reclaiming the earth which has been promised to the littles ones. Last year, some of them planted a garden, cared for it and shared its fruits. It stood before the whole street as a proclamation of return from exile.

The vision must be shared. Television crews come and ask questions, try to make sense of Wellspring. They catch a glimpse of something that excites them — this isn't just a "human interest" story about a beautiful old house and people providing shelter for pathetic women and children. This is somehow about how people live together, it is about reclaiming the earth. It is a song in a strange land, a song beginning to be heard, a song becoming the chant of returning exiles.

People from here — Mary Kay, Mary Jane, Donna, Nicole, Maura, Nell, Doris and the volunteers who are all part of the enterprise of Return — sit on committees, attend meetings of groups — of Shelter providers, of housing advocates, of a task force on teenage pregnancy. Nancy is asked to be President of the Massachusetts Coalition for the Homeless. All of us go to conferences, rallies, workshops. Twelve march with the 'Housing Now' demonstration in Washington. Some of this is boring, some of it is exasperating, some of it is exciting, some of it is tragic or naive or turns out to be just a "front' for political inertia, but much of it is full of goodness and hope. There *is* a network, people are learning.

(But one woman, once a homeless mother in a "Welfare hotel," now a community organizer, warned, "What we are doing is threatening to the powerful." She had realized, after several years, that she was recognizing some faces turning up in support groups for change in many parts of the country; they are faces of people paid to infiltrate, to disrupt, to provoke conflict, divide, discourage in whatever way possible to undermine the work of rebuilding. The forces of evil are not only powerful but intelligent and patient. They have their network too.)

When did we first begin to talk about a Community Land Trust?

I remember. We went to a gathering of the Green Party, that chaotic and yet inspiring collection of hopes and dreams, of elderly hippies and young educators, of environmentalists and mystics and demagogues and practical South American and German politicians, of angry farmers, and outdated and arrogant secular humanists and aristocratic Buddhists and outrageous comedians and ingenuous inventors and weavers and potters and poets and gardeners and Episcopal clergy and extra-liberated women with long grey hair and long skirts and semi-liberated nuns in shorts, with a sprinkling of gurus and even a few ordinary people. It was a muddle, broken by a few excellent, well thought out and well presented talks, some strange meals, propaganda for a sect or two and some very good displays of books and other things. We were housed, if that is the word, in college dorms of concrete and green paint, defaced, chipped and graffitied by the expensive middleclass young who normally inhabit them. The Green people, if disorganized, were at least undestructive and friendly.

Among thc exhibits was a display of the Institute for Community Economics. It was about Land Trusts. It was about coming home to the earth. We returned from the gathering with many ideas, and a sharpening of vision, with memories of laughter and of moving hopes. But we brought back also some books about Land Trusts. A year later Wellspring announced the creation of its own Land Trust.

A Community Land Trust is a non-profit corporation whose purpose is to acquire and administer land and housing. The point of it is that the Trust owns the land for as long as it (the Trust) exisits; but the houses on that land — existing or specially built — can be sold leasehold to people needing homes. Because they do not buy the land but only the house, because the Trust is non-profit and therefore pays no taxes, and is often eligible for grants towards either acquisition or building, and itself does not aim to make a profit, the Trust can sell houses at a price that even low-income people can afford. It can support owners' cooperatives, it can use (if it likes) "sweat equity." It can also be a landlord and rent, again at a lower rent than is usually possible.

A home owner can do what he or she or they like with the home — alter it, bequeath, enlarge it. If they want to sell, they may only sell it at the price they paid, plus adjustment for inflation and any improvements they have made, so it *remains* affordable. Thus, land and houses become places to live, not investments. The earth is God's, the earth is for people; with the help of the Land Trust, at least a few can come home. It turns on its head the value system of the property market, and fulfills the vision of the prophet: "they shall build houses, and live in them," — "and when they call, I shall answer even before they call." People who have come home are at home with the God who calls out of exile.

There really are practical ways to begin to reclaim the earth, to come home. There are ways to make the earth home. Our earth is called by the name of the Greek earth goddess, beautiful Gaia, floating in space, fragile, tough, complex. James Lovelock and others developed the "Gaia hypothesis", the theory that the earth functions as a single organism which defines and maintains the conditions for her own survival, an organism that, as Fridjof Capra has suggested, has what can only be called "mind — she can know" what she needs and must fear. The evidence is persuasive, fascinating and deeply moving, and both frightening and comforting. Most of all it makes clear that the work of human beings, for their own sake, is to respond with sensitivity and intelligence to the signs of Gaia's needs. Making earth a true home for humankind means understanding how all creation is at home with us. It is a delicate job of household management, — budgeting, storing for the future, healing wounds, cleaning, repairing, dealing with sibling rivalry and domestic crises, understanding the family history and making plans for the family future.

Women's work? In a sense yes. Certainly a job women can understand, a job that women are undertaking; it is a job for all humankind — but a "right brain" task. In "Gaia" James Lovelock says: "Part of our reward for fulfilling our biological role of creating a home and raising a family is the underlying sense of satisfaction. However hard and disappointing at the time the task may have been, we are still pleasurably aware at a deeper level of having played our proper part and stayed in the mainstream of life. We are equally and painfully aware of a sense of failure and loss if for some reason or other we have missed our way or made a mess of things.

"It may be that we are also programmed to recognize instinctively our optimal role in relation to other forms of life around us. When we act according to this instinct in our dealings with our partners in Gaia, we are rewarded by finding that what seems right also looks good and arouses those pleasurable feelings which comprise our sense of beauty. When this relationship with our environment is spoilt or mishandled, we suffer from a sense of emptiness and deprivation."

Human beings do have the ability to know the needs of the earth, which are our needs. We are able, even at this late date, to save our home and at the same time (because the two can't be separated) to make it truly a home for the dispossessed of the earth.

It seems that it takes disaster to bring about change in the minds of the powerful, but disaster opens them to the insights of those who have been willing to know, and to work for change. And it is sometimes disaster that can introduce a whole new element into the relationship of men and women as they face a common future. Something has happened, for instance, to men who help other men who have AIDS. The love of gay men for each other grows and changes as they take on the work of caring for their lovers who are dying, and their whole feeling about life is transformed. Other men get involved — as masseurs, as hospice workers, as home helpers, discovering among themselves the compassion — or the rage — which transforms. They meet women involved in the same work of caring. They do it together, and the encounters are like nothing they have known in male-female relationship. The women encounter men who are tender, vulnerable, not afraid to grieve, men who know about life because they have braved their own deaths, overcoming fear. The men meet women as friends, sharing grief, learning together to look forward beyond death, to envision a better earth, where such shared homemaking is not an exception but the common enterprise.

Like the men and women who mourned Jesus, and began together to build a different community because he had overcome death, these are people who are changed. The earliest resurrection community felt this same deep fellowship and saw itself called to a new creation.

Sadly, it doesn't often happen, but it can happen. Men and women are called together, but it remains, for the present, especially women's work, for the sake of all. The women know how, and the women know that the task of earthly homemaking is also the only way they themselves can come home. Conversely, the return home of the dispossessed, most of whom are women, is also how the earth herself may have a future, is also what Jesus was calling people to create: a new heaven and a new earth, which the humble are to inherit.

Wellspring is one tiny, growing, obstinate, erratic little entity, learning skills and dealing with emotions and cooking and cleaning up (in every sense). Home-making, so that the land may be home to all. The song we sing (sometimes out of tune, or fitfully, sometimes quite loud and clear) is indeed a song in a strange land, because we are exiles, but we are trying to change that, to come home, with all the others who have no home; then the song will be different, it will be a song of harvest home. Just to be sure, we are practicing it already. It will be a song for a mixed chorus, of course. Meanwhile, after all, home-making *is* women's work.